LAWRENCE A. RUBIN

BRIDGING the STRAITS

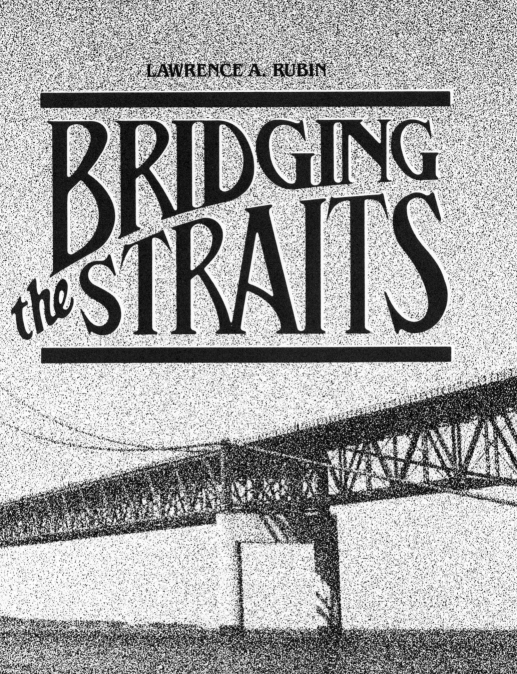

The Story of Mighty Mac

WAYNE STATE UNIVERSITY PRESS   DETROIT 1985

Library of Congress Cataloging in Publication Data

Rubin, Lawrence A.
  Bridging the Straits.

  Includes index.
  1. Mackinac Bridge (Mich.) 2. Michigan—Politics
and government—1951–   . I. Title.
HE376.M3R83   1985   388.1′32′0977488   85–11475
ISBN 0–8143–1789–8

To the men who lost their lives
during the construction of the
Mackinac Bridge

Frank Pepper
James R. LeSarge
Albert B. Abbott
Jack C. Baker
Robert Koppen

CONTENTS

Contents

4
THE THREE WISE MEN

5
THE HUNTING LICENSE

6
VAN INGEN IS CONFIDENT

7
A NATURAL DISASTER

8
EMIL PELTZ SAVES THE DAY

9
A NEW PITCH

10
JIM ABRAMS'S OFFER

11
HOW LIFE INSURANCE COMPANIES PROVIDE LIFE

Contents

ix

Contents

What They Wrought

ILLUSTRATIONS

Illustrations

James S. Abrams, Jr.

*The delivery of the bonds and check presentation ceremony,
February 17, 1954*

*Herman Ellis, Mackinac Bridge photographer,
atop the uncompleted bridge*

Engineers measuring the angle of H-beams

*Pre-opening inspection tour of the Mackinac Bridge,
November 1, 1957*

*John C. Mackie, Steinman, Governor G. Mennen Williams,
and Authority members on bridge*

*Grover Denny, George A. Osborn, Steinman,
and Herbert Goodkind*

*Brown receives album of Mackinac Bridge
commemorative stamps from
Postmaster General Arthur Summerfield*

Jack Kinney and David B. Steinman

*The chain link fence platform is prepared
for cable spinning*

Ellis on the tower of the bridge

Ellis focusing for a publicity photograph

*Lights strung on the bridge for around-the-clock
cable spinning*

*Governor George Romney and the author
participating in the 1966 Bridge Walk*

FOREWORD

During the preconstruction bridge period described in this book, my father, Prentiss M. Brown, praised the efforts of Governor Williams and the members he appointed to the Bridge Authority. However, most particularly, he singled out Charles T. Fisher, Jr., Governor Van Wagoner, and Larry Rubin for their efforts, with him, to complete the financing of the bridge. He also expressed great confidence in David B. Steinman and Jim Abrams. But what I recall most vividly was his reaction to the rejections and trials that he faced and which are set forth in this book. He could not hide from my brothers and sisters, nor my mother, the drain it had upon him. He always bounced back, however. Somewhere the determination he possessed would be rekindled, probably from the basic truth he often expressed—that the bridge across the Straits was an absolutely worthy and feasible project.

Through his long and varied career, there was always the determination to do something about a permanent link connecting Michigan's two peninsulas. It was not for lack of effort that the bridge was not built in the twenties and thirties. It seems that fate decreed that it would be built in the twilight of my father's life. Thus, in view of his many successes during his most productive years, his diary entry of February 17, 1954, becomes ever so much more meaningful.

New York   Bridge Money
                                                          February 17, 1954
This is the big day—up early and left at 7:40 with Mom and Pat to Bankers Trust at 9:45. All Bridge Authority there but Ziegler. Joe King of Union Securities gave me the check for $96,400,033.33 and the long battle for the money was over. Persistence, fight, cajolery, determination, friendship, force on reluctant people, hard work, discouragement, hope and I will say ability and finally constant prayer in the late stages put it over. My greatest public accomplishment.

This book which you are about to read is of great historical importance. It is an exciting political history, not heretofore told. It should be required reading for all history and political science students as an example of how to persevere in planning and completing a significant public project.

St. Ignace, Michigan   Prentiss M. Brown, Jr.

PREFACE

The seeds from which this book grew were planted February 17, 1954. That was the day the Mackinac Bridge Authority received a check for $96,400,033.33, the proceeds of the sale of Mackinac Bridge bonds. Up to that time, whenever I was called upon to speak about the proposed bridge, I promoted the project and the need for it with facts and figures guaranteeing its physical and financial feasibility.

But once the construction funds were in hand, I began to talk about the trials and tribulations of obtaining them. Much to my amazement and pleasure, the audiences seemed to love it. Young or old, male or female, blue-collar or white-collar, they were fascinated by the story of the Bridge Authority overcoming the many obstacles with which it was faced.

If people, I thought, are so interested in this material, why not put it in a book? But for the next twenty-five years I had my hands full with running the Mackinac Bridge, and so the book became a retirement project. In my retirement, it promptly became a labor of love.

My purpose in writing this book was threefold: first, to let it be known that failure to finance the bridge lived with the Authority; success visited once, and once was enough; second, to fill in a few pages of history crediting those persons whose substantial contributions to the project have hitherto been unrecognized; and finally, to illustrate how through perseverance, faith, and courage, difficult—and seemingly impossible—obstacles can be overcome.

It is my intent to report in detail the events from 1950 to 1957 that led to the opening of the Mackinac Bridge. Excellent histories have been written about the Mackinac Bridge, some of which go back to 1884 to document when the idea of a permanent link joining the two peninsulas first seems to have appeared. The late Frank B. Woodford's introduction to *Mighty Mac: The Official Picture History of the Mackinac Bridge*, written by your author and published by Wayne State University Press, covers the story of the Straits from the time of the glaciers to the dedication of the bridge. Then, there is Willard Baird's history pamphlet published by the *Sault Ste. Marie Evening News*, and more recently my brochure *The Story of the Mackinac Bridge* published by the Bridge Twenty-Fifth Anniversary Committee.

This book was written from the point of view of the Mackinac Bridge Authority. Had it been written by Allen & Company, the principal underwriter, a legislator, or a member of the governor's staff, it might very well have emphasized a different aspect or view of the struggle to build the bridge. History often depends upon the perch from which the observer reports the battle. Thus, all the heroes who participated in the struggle may not have been given their due. The earlier efforts of former governor Murray D. Van Wagoner and state highway commissioner G. Donald Kennedy, engineers James Cissell, William Housel, John H. McCarthy, and William McLaughlin come to mind. Others include the late George E. Bishop, Governor Chase S. Osborn and former governor G. Mennen Williams. The Mackinac Bridge probably would not have become a reality in 1957, or for the foreseeable future, had not Williams been governor during the crucial years of its incubation.

In being truthful about the whole story, I might have hurt the feelings of or embarrassed some persons who placed stumbling blocks in the path of progress. If I have, I regret it. It had to be done in order to tell the truth.

The events I describe are factual or based on fact. Wherever possible, I researched such documents as the Mackinac Bridge Authority minutes, correspondence, and reports; the journals of the Michigan House of Representatives and Senate; Prentiss M. Brown's diaries on file at the Bentley Memorial Library of the University of Michigan; newspaper and magazine clippings; the consulting engineers' daily and monthly reports of construction; and numerous other publications.

Also, I conducted interviews over the years with many persons whose cooperation I gratefully acknowledge: W. Stewart Woodfill; G. Donald Kennedy; Murray D. Van Wagoner; James S. Abrams, Jr.; former member of the House of Representatives Gerald Graves, who participated in the caucus described in the chapter about Emil Peltz; and W. Palmer Carr, who was a deputy to State Treasurer D. Hale Brake. Obviously, the conversations related in this book were not electronically or otherwise recorded, but, with literary license, the essence of what was said and what took place is honestly reported.

I am grateful to many individuals who helped with the preparation of this book: Prentiss M. Brown, Jr., for writing the Foreword; Dan Musser for the line drawings of the Grand Hotel as it originally appeared; Stellanova Osborn and Ann Pratt for the letter describing Governor Osborn's meetings with President Roosevelt; the people at Wayne State University Press who were so receptive and helpful: Director Bernard M. Goldman, Associate Director Richard Kinney, Editor-in-Chief Jean Owen, and Editor Anne M. G. Adamus.

My wife, Olga, deserves thanks for tolerating an impossible daily schedule while I was engaged in research and writing, and for deciphering my hen tracks to type the correspondence related to this book. Finally, I acknowledge with great pleasure and pride the assistance provided by my son, David, who critiqued my writing, made valuable suggestions, and committed the entire manuscript to a word processor.

Bankers, Lawyers, and Politicians

In the Beginning

Prentiss M. Brown, former U.S. senator, chairman of the Mackinac Bridge Authority, was driving from Detroit to Lansing where, on the following day, December 17, 1953, a seventy-year struggle to finance the building of a bridge across the Straits of Mackinac would be successfully concluded.

As a child growing up in St. Ignace, the northern terminus of the proposed bridge, he had visualized and dreamed of a magnificent structure over the Straits. As a young county prosecutor and budding politician, he strongly advocated the Straits crossing. As a U.S. congressman he had introduced legislation requesting permission from the Corps of Engineers to build a bridge. He had served as legal counsel for the Mackinac Straits Bridge Authority, established in 1934 and abolished in 1947, and in 1950, when a new authority was created, he was elected chairman.

During the past three years, he had worked tirelessly—in addition to his duties as chairman of the board of the Detroit Edison Company, one of the nation's largest power companies—for the realization of his lifelong dream: the Mackinac Bridge. Now that dream was about to become reality. At ten o'clock the next morning, the Mackinac Bridge Authority would offer to sell and accept bids on $99,800,000 worth of bonds. The procedure would be pro forma, governed by the legislation enabling the Authority to finance, build, and operate the bridge. Accordingly, the invitation to bid was open to all, but in this instance there would be only one. Details had been worked out in advance. The leader of the syndicate bidding on the bonds would give Chairman Brown a good-faith check for $100,000 guaranteeing their intent to sell the bonds and deliver the proceeds. That would take place in about two months. Then, contracts could be implemented and construction could begin.

Brown's wife, Marian, disturbed his reverie to tell him that it was nearly time for the 1:00 P.M. news. He clicked on the car radio.

"Today Senator Haskell L. Nichols, Republican from Jackson, petitioned the Supreme Court to prohibit the sale of one-hundred-million dollars of Mackinac Bridge bonds scheduled for bid opening tomorrow. Senator Nichols told reporters that he wanted to test the validity of the legislation earmarking motor vehicle highway funds for bridge operation, maintenance, and repair.

"In other news from Lansing today. . . . "

The car swerved onto the shoulder and the wheels hit the snowbank along the drainage ditch, but Brown, the former semipro baseball player, retained his sharp reflexes and steadied the vehicle, the only damage being his wife's distress.

"Prentiss, be careful!"

Brown knew the impact of a decision by the court to grant Nichols's petition. He was not about to let a seventy-year battle be lost without fighting back. Known for his tenacity as well as his legal sagacity, he began to plan his counterattack.

He apologized for his poor driving and then explained what Nichols was trying to do. "If the bond sale is not completed tomorrow, it will have to be postponed, because of the Christmas holiday, until after December 31, 1953, a crucial date. Last April, the legislature grudgingly appropriated an annual $417,000 to the Bridge Authority for the operation, maintenance, and repair of the bridge, if it is built and opened for traffic. It was a conditional gesture to convince prospective bond buyers that the state has a stake in the bridge. But the lawmakers attached a second restriction: the bonds must be sold by December 31, or the appropriation will expire. If this happens, prospective bond purchasers will lose interest.

"The announcer," Brown continued, "reported that Nichols wanted to test the validity of the legislative appropriation. He had seven months to petition the court, but he waited until the day before the sale of the bonds. Indeed, Marian, I question his motive and I think the justices will, too."

2

The Innkeeper

By far, Michigan's best-known travel attraction is Mackinac Island. And the island's foremost attraction is the Grand Hotel, the center of a vast landscape of formal gardens, tennis courts, a golf course, stables, a pool, fountains, and miscellaneous service buildings—a fiefdom dominated for nearly a half century by the late William Stewart Woodfill, who preferred the British affectation, "W. Stewart."

In his time, this self-styled "Innkeeper" played host to international celebrities from the worlds of politics, society, entertainment, and the arts. He strutted about his domain nightly, black book in hand, making notes for the next morning's instructions. His employees performed with a "snap-to-it" discipline that would win the admiration of a suzerain.

Jack Benny, the famous comedian, once deigned to come to the island with several friends unannounced and without reservations. There were no rooms available at the Grand, and even Woodfill's lovely home on the island was already occupied by over-booked guests. The best that could be obtained for the celebrity was a bedroom at one of the hostelries in dire need of remodeling.

Benny and his friends were guests of Woodfill at dinner

that evening. There was a good deal of banter about Benny's accommodations. Benny remarked that he had just returned from Holland where Queen Wilhelmina placed one of her castles at his disposal. Woodfill stated that he was impressed, but added in a friendly, yet imperious manner, that it did not change his rule: "No reservations, no rooms." Benny good-humoredly joked about Woodfill's autocracy and referred to him as "Senator Woodfill" for the rest of the evening.

W. Stewart Woodfill decided in 1949 that the time was ripe for building the Mackinac Bridge. The Mackinac Straits Bridge Authority, having been disbanded in 1947, would have to be revived. The legislature would have to be persuaded to establish a new authority—and only a couple of years after they killed the first one. Legislators don't fancy such turnabouts. That would not deter Woodfill, tall, erect, meticulously attired, and hair slickly "coifed" (to use his own term). Always with a walking stick, not a cane ("a cane is for the lame") and thick, tortoise-shell-rimmed glasses for reading, he had a deep resonant voice that he used with consummate oratorical, if not theatrical, skill. He was a master of persuasive argument and could readily convince skeptics sitting around a conference table. He was an equally skilled and indefatigable organizer.

He needed a vehicle for his bridge legislation promotion, so he created the Mackinac Bridge Citizens Committee. It was comprised of prominent citizens from all over the state. As owner of the Grand Hotel, he was owed many favors—due bills he planned to call in. Public sentiment was strong for a permanent, year-round crossing at the Straits of Mackinac, if it could be built and financed without being a burden to the state. Governor G. Mennen Williams had made the bridge a campaign issue in his 1948 upset victory over incumbent Kim Sigler.

Ten years earlier, Governor Murray D. Van Wagoner and State Highway Commissioner G. Donald Kennedy had pressed ahead with plans for the project. If World War II had not interfered, the bridge would have been built at that time.

Van Wagoner, Kennedy, and Williams were Democrats, and Woodfill, always the pragmatist, noted, in his early correspondence to prospective committee members, that because of the Democratic tinge associated with the bridge, the committee ought to be loaded with "people of unquestionable Republican faith, but who are advocates of the bridge being built." So it was that in 1949, eleven distinguished Michigan citizens, from Detroit to Houghton and from St. Joseph to Sault Ste. Marie, were persuaded by Woodfill, as chairman, to serve on his newly formed committee, with headquarters in Detroit.

Several months after his inauguration in January 1949, Governor Williams established the Inter-Peninsula Communications Commission. He appointed John McCarthy, chairman of the State Public Service Commission, as chairman. The main thrust of the new commission was to establish closer commercial, governmental, social, and cultural ties between the Upper and Lower Peninsulas. Its mission also included overcoming the barrier to such communication at the Straits, which created a sense of isolation and prompted Upper Peninsula residents to feel closer to Wisconsin than to lower Michigan.

McCarthy served ably as chairman of the State Public Service Commission, although the senate, led by hard-core Republicans, never confirmed his appointment. The strategists were convinced that Governor Williams would be defeated in the next election. Then, the new governor could appoint a chairman more to their liking. As it turned out, "Soapy" Williams won six elections in a row, more than any other governor in Michigan history, and McCarthy served as Public Service Commission chairman for twelve years, even though his appointment was never approved by the senate.

The senate's refusal to accept McCarthy limited his Inter-Peninsula Communications activities largely to Democratic lobbying for a peninsular link and left open a vast area of Republican political pasturage for Woodfill's committee to feed upon. It was important to prevent the bridge project from becoming a one-party affair.

Woodfill was a prolific letter writer and a competent after-dinner speaker. Both attributes served his committee well. Critical editorials and letters to editors he answered quickly, clearly, and with sound rebuttal. He traveled the roast chicken and mashed potatoes circuit diligently. He imparted irrefutable facts and figures about the proposed bridge, cited correspondence with the nation's foremost engineers confirming his opinion that a bridge could be built at the Straits, and did not hesitate to call or write anybody, no matter how prominent, if he thought the result might be favorable publicity or deflection of public criticism of his efforts.

Early on, however, he ran into an obstacle: Dr. Kenneth K. Landes, chairman of the University of Michigan Geology Department. Professor Landes and two of his colleagues studied the rock formations underlying the Straits in 1944. In his report, made public in 1949, Landes disclosed that in his view a suspension bridge over the Straits of Mackinac could lead to a "possible disaster of shocking proportions." All three geologists were convinced that the rock formations in the straits region could not support the terrific weight of the four-mile span.

Woodfill went after Landes. No recordings or memos were kept of their conversations, but I can well imagine Woodfill lecturing Landes about the fact that he was a geologist, not a bridge engineer. Nearly a year after their confrontation, Woodfill summed up the dispute, in a letter published in the *Iron Mountain News*, on October 14, 1950.

Landes was the best authority on Mackinac Straits geology, Woodfill wrote, and was sincere in stating a year earlier that a safe bridge could not be built, but he had since changed his mind. Woodfill admitted that Landes was still worried about the cost, but noted that Landes's expertise as a geologist would be of great value in solving the foundation problem. "It will primarily be a matter for study of engineering-geologists and great bridge engineers, and this very fine citizen and top-flight geologist, Professor Landes, readily attests to that."

Having disposed of the Landes matter, Woodfill's committee then directed its efforts to the legislature. It was in special session, which meant it would adjourn before planting season. Thus, time was of the essence. Some bridge backers, Woodfill and Williams included, thought the authority to be created ought to be enabled to finance, build, and operate the bridge, providing feasibility studies proved it could be accomplished without placing any financial burden whatsoever on the state or any of its agencies, such as the Highway Department. Woodfill presented a convincing argument for an authority that could get something done and not be just another study committee producing a report to gather dust.

Others felt that giving a newly created authority too much power would alienate conservative members of the legislature, many of whom, from both parties, had sincere doubts about the bridge. They wanted to proceed one step at a time. First, find out once and for all whether or not a bridge could be built at the Straits of Mackinac that would be strong enough to withstand all the challenges of nature, such as winds, currents, and ice, and surmount the rock formations and depths involved. Next, determine the cost of such a structure. Third, conduct studies to learn if traffic growth and subsequent revenues would be sufficient to repay all the costs of construction and upkeep. Finally, rely only on the advice of the foremost experts for the necessary information.

To obtain this kind of expertise would be expensive. As a result, the legislation proposed by Woodfill's committee, which was prepared by one of the nation's leading legal firms specializing in revenue bond law, called for all the aforementioned work to be paid for out of state highway funds which would be reimbursed from the proceeds of the sale of bridge bonds. That is where Woodfill met his match. Here is an excerpt from his report to his committee, April 3, 1950:

> Senator William C. Vandenburg of Holland is chairman of the Senate State Affairs Committee. On March 24 I wrote

to him asking if it would be possible for me to appear before
him and his Committee and explain what I had learned from
the extensive studies given to this matter. He replied three
days ago stating that WHEN AND IF the committee should decide to hold any hearings on this Bill, or this matter, he would
let me know. . . . He told me that the Bill was wholly unac-
ceptable. . . . I inquired what changes he desired in the bill,
what it might be that was objectionable to him. He stated . . .
that the Legislature was not going to authorize one penny of
funds from the Highway Department or any other source to
study and investigate building this bridge, and that at the
most he would be opposed to anything but a study commission and that only if someone other than the State advanced
the funds to study the project. . . . We need all the pressure
possible to be brought to bear upon Senator Vandenburg . . .
to grant us a hearing on the Bill. Please do what you can to
secure that and advise and help me if you please in any way
that you can. Our bridge campaign has hit a serious snag.

Vandenburg, a round-faced, no-necked, barrel-chested
bale of solidity, was no more likely to be moved by Woodfill's
blandishments than by his blustering. When he looked over
his rimless glasses and softly said "No," it was no! Hundreds
of letters written to him at the instigation of the Citizens
Committee did not move him.

During the next six weeks the meetings, the compro-
mises, and the pressure to accomplish something during the
current session of the legislature resulted in a modified proposal that was more or less acceptable to all concerned. It
was more acceptable to Williams and Woodfill, who above all
wanted a new authority created, and to conservative members of the legislature who opposed any appropriation to the
authority. It was less acceptable to those who wanted a mul-
timillion-dollar appropriation and to their strange bedfel-
lows who were opposed to the bridge legislation entirely.

The new bill was introduced in the House of Representatives where it was passed by a vote of eighty-seven to one.
It then went to the senate where the presiding officer sent it
to the Highways Committee, bypassing Vandenburg's State
Affairs Committee. The bill was passed in the senate with a
unanimous vote. Senator Vandenburg was absent.

In his final report to his committee, Woodfill wrote:

> My hearty thanks to all of you for your service on the committee and for your confidence so frequently demonstrated in my leadership of this undertaking. The list of contributors remains the same as shown in my last report of contributions. All accounts have been paid in full. Our work is finished and it was a success. The committee is hereby dissolved.

He celebrated too soon.

3

Luck Breeds Opportunity

June 6, 1950, promised to be a day no different from any other. As executive director of the Michigan Good Roads Federation, I basically carried on a publicity and promotion campaign to win grass roots support for the proposed legislation that would fulfill Michigan's highway needs.

Most lawmakers and the executive office, sensitive to public opinion, were concerned with the two recommended amendments to increase gasoline and weight taxes. Five additional bills suggested were noncontroversial and would truly modernize highway, road, and street administration. Thoroughfares would be classified according to the service they provided, and registered professional engineers would be hired to fill positions that demanded engineering expertise. It was a good program—and long overdue.

It was presented to Governor Sigler in December 1948. He had promised to "carry the ball" for good roads in Michigan, but he stumbled. According to knowledgeable sources the governor skimmed through the 165-page study report, called in the chief correspondent for one of the newspaper chains, and the two decided that the best way to meet Michigan's highway needs was to double the tax on trucks, an oversimplified as well as impractical solution to a complicated problem.

Capitol pundits claim this high-handed treatment of the highway, road, and street interests cost the governor his re-election nine months later. It didn't help, either, that the county road commissioners, closely aligned with the Republican-dominated "courthouse gang," simply did not totally support the top man on their ticket. Thus, the young, handsome, handshaking, square-dance calling, and one-on-one campaigning G. Mennen Williams upset the incumbent and carried along John Connolly as lieutenant governor and Stephen Roth as attorney general.

It was Williams's chief of staff who called me about 2:00 P.M. on that fateful day of June 6. Although none of the Good Roads bills were faring well, the legislature did pass an act enabling the Highway Department to issue bonds, the proceeds of which would be used to build expressways in and around Detroit. I played a part in promoting this legislation.

"Larry, the governor's having a bill-signing ceremony tomorrow in connection with S.B. 35 and we wanted your input regarding who should participate."

"I'll be right over," I replied, since the capitol was only a block or so away and I always welcomed any excuse to get out of the office. Also, I enjoyed visiting with Larry Farrell, the governor's executive secretary, with whom I had worked after World War II in the Office of Price Administration, when Williams was the administration's deputy director in Michigan.

It didn't take long to make out the list for the next day's ceremony, and I was about to leave when I saw some old acquaintances milling around the area adjacent to the executive office. There was Murray D. ("Pat") Van Wagoner, former governor and state highway commissioner, for whom I worked for nearly five years prior to December 1941; Prentiss M. Brown, who remembered me from his first (and successful) campaign for the U.S. Senate in 1936 and was now chairman of the board of the Detroit Edison Company; and Wood-fill, who was chatting with the few members of the press present. Woodfill and I had spent several hours together a few weeks earlier in the House Gallery discussing his committee's work while watching and waiting for the third and final reading of the bill that would establish a bridge authority.

It was then that I realized that this bill, creating the Mackinac Bridge Authority, was about to be signed by the governor in a formal picture-taking ceremony. The door to the executive office opened and Governor Williams greeted each man most cordially with a personal comment about the individual or his family. He spoke in that slightly louder than normal voice he naturally used for such occasions.

I thought I had better watch this ceremony so that I would have some idea of what to expect the next day when S.B. 35 would be signed into law.

It was not an elaborate affair. The governor signed twelve copies of Public Act 21 of the Public Acts of 1950, each time with a different pen (those were the days of wooden holders and steel nibs). The holders were then notched, and "P.A. 21" was printed in the notch. All of those present gathered behind the governor, who gave each of them a pen, and everybody said "cheese" as the flashbulbs popped (those were also the days before strobe lights).

Again I was about to leave when I saw a half dozen of the persons present seat themselves around a table connected to the governor's desk. I knew then that the governor had already appointed a bridge authority, and the members were about to conduct their first meeting.

I decided to watch this historic event. After all, the project was not new or strange to me. In 1940 I had helped draft a presentation to be made to President Roosevelt designed to win his support and some New Deal money for the bridge and had journeyed to Washington with then State Highway Commissioner G. Donald Kennedy who, despite his inordinate persuasive powers and convincing arguments, came away emptyhanded.

The first thing the Authority did was elect Brown temporary chairman. I scanned the news release handed out by the governor's press secretary and took note of the membership of the body: Charles T. Fisher, Jr., was named vice-chairman. He was the son of one of the famous Fisher brothers of the Fisher Body Corporation, president of the National Bank of Detroit, the nation's fourth largest, and a director of many large corporations, including General Motors. There was also Fred M. Zeder, vice-chairman of the Chrysler Corporation; George A. Osborn, publisher of the *Sault Ste. Marie Evening News* and son of the famous Chase S. Osborn, former governor and pioneer bridge promoter; Van Wagoner, who in his former capacity as highway commissioner is credited with giving Michigan the best highway system in the nation; William J. Cochran, General Motors dealer and banker; and Charles M. Ziegler, state highway commissioner, served as an ex officio member.

This was truly a blue-ribbon commission. Usually such bodies have one or more "politicals" appointed to pay off political debts. Not this group. The law required three Republicans and three Democrats be appointed, but none of these were professional partisans. It is true that Brown and Van Wagoner had been elected to office on the Democratic ticket, but that was long ago and they were now considered elder statesmen.

Clearly Governor Williams was going to avoid the pitfall that had plagued the previous authority and earlier efforts to promote the bridge. Williams would not allow the bridge issue to become a "political football," as it had been called in the past. All of the six men appointed by the governor could be depended upon not to play politics with the project.

I decided to watch a little longer. The next order of business was to appoint a secretary who by law could have been a member of the Authority, but apparently it was understood that an outside executive would better fill the position.

Osborn suggested Ralph Swan, who was then director of Public Information for the State Highway Department. But Highway Commissioner Ziegler, whose opposition to a bridge was already a matter of public record, stated that Swan was too busy to take on any additional assignments and could not be made available.

Osborn did not take this opposition too kindly and persisted with his recommendation. Ziegler was just as stubborn and it looked as though the Authority's first meeting would be a rocky one. But Brown, an old hand at presiding over squabbles, put out the fire before it blazed and appointed Van Wagoner and Ziegler as a committee of two to investigate and recommend a candidate for secretary at the next meeting.

I was becoming more and more interested. As executive director of the Michigan Good Roads Federation, I was well aware of the opposition to our legislation by the automobile company lobbyists. And here, on this Authority, were Fisher, General Motors director; Zeder, Chrysler vice-chairman; and Cochran, General Motors distributor. What a fine opportunity: If I could get the ears of these three men I could do a lot of good for the federation program.

When the meeting broke up I approached Van Wagoner and Ziegler individually. Both were directors of the Michigan Good Roads Federation and knew me well. I volunteered to handle the duties of Authority secretary and even offered to serve without pay.

It is interesting to note that Van Wagoner and Ziegler disliked each other about as much as any civilized men could. But on June 24, 1950, at the first official meeting of the Mackinac Bridge Authority on Mackinac Island, they were in agreement and recommended that I be appointed secretary. The members concurred unanimously. As Woodfill observed to me several weeks later: "It was the only thing those two ever agreed on in their whole lives."

The Three Wise Men

Even before passage of the act creating the Authority, Woodfill was making recommendations to Governor Williams regarding Authority membership. He sought no position for himself—possibly because he was not a registered voter in Michigan, although this situation easily could have been changed if he were ambitious to serve. Instead he studied the backgrounds and reputations of scores of persons and recommended several Republicans and Democrats who could be depended upon not to play politics with the project. Governor Williams looked over Woodfill's suggestions and, considering them with his own choice of candidates, appointed the best commission possible. However, as the years went by, Woodfill would say with pardonable exaggeration that he had named the original bridge authority.

The Authority members were confirmed by the senate less than two weeks after the appointments were made. In that short time span, however, two unofficial meetings were held: the one I observed on June 6, 1950, the day the legislation was signed by the governor, and the other on June 20, 1950, to establish the ground rules for the first official meeting to be held on June 24, 1950, on Mackinac Island.

18

At this first official meeting, Brown's status as temporary chairman of the Authority was changed to permanent. Brown then appointed Zeder, Van Wagoner, and Ziegler, who were engineers, as a committee to negotiate with the prospective bridge designers. The final order of business was a motion by Highway Commissioner Ziegler, seconded by Fisher, "that the Authority retain Mr. Lawrence A. Rubin as Secretary of the Authority at a rate of $10,000 per year, but that only one quarter of his time would be required, therefore his pay would be $2,500 per year plus necessary expenses." The motion carried unanimously.

The Mackinac Bridge Authority's first task was to determine whether or not a bridge could be built across the Straits of Mackinac that would withstand and overcome all the forces of nature. The legislation creating the Authority required that three of the nation's leading bridge designers be retained to study in great detail the geology and geography of the Straits: the distance between shores, the nature of the underlying material on which the foundations would be built, the velocities of the winds and currents, and the depth, movement, and pressure of the ice. Based on their findings, they would then decide what type of structure would be required to bridge the Straits and provide an estimate of the cost of that structure.

The Authority was empowered only to determine the feasibility of a bridge. Governor Williams, Woodfill, and John McCarthy agreed early that if the matter were to be kept out of politics and if the critics were to be refuted, the Authority would need impartial expert knowledge and advice.

The legislation also required that the dean of the University of Michigan School of Engineering recommend nationally renowned long-span bridge engineers to advise and consult with the Authority regarding the physical and financial feasibility of the project. Dean Ivan Crawford submitted his list of the nation's ten top engineers to the Authority at the same meeting at which I was hired as executive secretary. Zeder, chairman of the Authority's engineering committee, invited the first three on the list to meet with the Authority

19

at their earliest convenience to discuss whether or not they would serve, and, if so, what their remuneration would be.

The Authority expected that it would be a month to six weeks before a meeting with the engineers could be arranged, so I decided to take a vacation in July at Narragansett Pier, Rhode Island. That is where I was on July 10, an overcast day, unsuitable for the beach but possibly good for fishing. I picked up some bait at about noon and dropped by the hotel for my tackle only to find a wire from my secretary stating that there would be a meeting of the Authority on Wednesday, July 12, at the Grand Hotel on Mackinac Island—about a thousand miles away. As there was no direct plane service between Narragansett and Mackinac Island, I decided to drive. I left at about 2:30 P.M. and drove until well past midnight when, overcome by sleepiness, I stopped in the Finger Lake country of New York at a tourist home for a few hours of rest. The next day, I arrived at the Straits, spent the night in Mackinaw City, and made the early boat to the island, arriving in time for the meeting.

Well, they were there—the nation's three leading long-span bridge engineers and designers. One was Othmar H. Ammann, a Swiss-born New Yorker, tall, taciturn, sixtyish, who had an angular face and wore thick, horn-rimmed glasses. He spoke in his heavily accented, deep voice with conviction and self-assurance. His overall impression on me was one of discipline—Prussian discipline. Ammann headed a firm reputed to be the foremost among designers of long-span bridges. He was responsible for designing such monumental structures as the George Washington and Whitestone bridges in New York and scores of others throughout the country.

Another was David B. Steinman, Brooklyn-born, short, and of a small-boned frame. He was also in his sixties, professional in manner, and although he spoke with a voice that cracked, it carried strong conviction. His early responses made it clear that he stood in the shadow of no man—at least no engineer. He likewise headed a prestigious firm. Many of his colleagues considered him a mathematical, if somewhat controversial, genius. He made it clear that he had designed or consulted on the design of some four hundred structures all over the world.

From the West Coast came the third designer, Glenn B. Woodruff of San Francisco. He was of a slightly different cut. Tall, slouchy, and handicapped by a speech impediment, he nevertheless made it known that his credentials were as good as his colleagues. Woodruff had participated in the design of several structures in the San Francisco area, including the Oakland Bay Bridge, which was eight miles long, had two major spans and foundations of record depths. His manner was less stern, and, in my judgment, he made less of an effort trying to impress the members of the Authority.

The legislature had appropriated $100,000 to the Authority to determine the physical and financial feasibility of the bridge. After a discussion by the members of what they expected of the engineers, Chairman Brown suggested that the engineers meet privately to draft a proposal for the Authority. An hour or so later, they offered the following agreement:

1. The Authority would retain a firm of traffic engineers with high reputations in financial circles to make an analysis and projection of the future traffic across the Straits of Mackinac.
2. The Authority would employ local crews to make whatever field surveys were deemed necessary by the consultants.
3. The Authority would undertake the borings at the Straits, which the consultants would supervise and interpret.
4. The consultants would submit a progress report in January 1951.
5. The consultants would in March or April 1951 submit a final report containing recommendations for the location, design, and structure of the bridge, and provide estimates of its costs.
6. In return for these services, a fee of $75,000, or

$25,000 each, would be expected. The consultants would meet all their own traveling and business expenses incident to the fulfillment of their responsibility to the Authority.

The Authority unanimously adopted a resolution accepting the engineers' proposal. Chairman Brown and Fisher were given the responsibility of retaining the traffic engineers. The next day Ammann, Steinman, and Woodruff journeyed to Lansing to examine the data in the Highway Department files pertaining to a Straits crossing. The Authority legislation required that such material be made available.

Sponsors of that legislation had known that without it, the data might be difficult to obtain. Highway Commissioner Ziegler was personally, professionally, and politically opposed to bridging the Straits of Mackinac. As the operator of the Straits ferry service, he had committed millions of dollars to the construction of the new ferry and to dock improvement. As an engineer, he was convinced that no structure could withstand the forces of nature at the Straits. And as a Republican, he was almost paranoid in his opposition to Governor Williams and former governor Van Wagoner, both Democrats and two of the strongest proponents of the bridge.

Notwithstanding, he hastily arranged for a press conference in his office at the request of several capital correspondents who were informed that the engineers would be in Lansing. Ammann, Steinman, and Woodruff fielded their questions with relative ease, and Ziegler established his public position in which he was in favor of a bridge, if it could be built to withstand all the forces of nature at the Straits and at a cost that would make it self-sufficient and not a drain on public funds. He was professional enough not to express his private opinion.

Ammann responded rather crisply to a question about the possibility of overcoming all of the problems imposed by nature at the Straits. He said, "Give us enough money and we can design a bridge that can reach to the moon." But clearest in my mind and one I shall always remember is the reply Steinman gave in response to a question posed by Owen Dietrich, the *Detroit Free Press*'s capital correspondent. Dietrich asked, "Gentlemen, what would happen to one of your foundations if a boat loaded with ore crashed into it?"

Steinman answered without a pause: "The boat would sink with a serious loss of life."

5

The Hunting License

The Authority met again on September 15, 1950, and adopted a resolution hiring Coverdale & Colpitts, a traffic engineering consulting firm from New York City, to make an analysis of Straits traffic and predict what it would be if the bridge were built. A letter was received from the three consulting engineers stating that progress was being made toward their filing a preliminary report in January; also, they recommended that an engineering geologist be retained to advise the Authority regarding the bedrock at the bottom of the Straits and its load-bearing capacity. (Professor Landes still had some reservations about his agreement with Woodfill and again raised the question about the stability of the bedrock at the Straits. To put the matter firmly to rest, an engineering geologist was hired.) At this time, the Authority directed the engineers to also consider railroad-carrying capacity in their bridge design and to estimate how much more it would cost.

The Authority received three heartening reports at its official meeting on January 10, 1951: the consulting engineers' report that a bridge could be built over the Straits of

Mackinac; the traffic engineers' report that if the cost of such a bridge were financed through the sale of revenue bonds to be redeemed with toll revenues, it would be self-liquidating in forty years; and a positive report of Charles P. Berkey, engineering geologist, regarding the rock formations at the Straits. In connection with the last report it may be interesting to describe a meeting which I attended that took place in Professor Landes's office in Ann Arbor shortly after the Authority had retained Berkey.

Present were Steinman, Woodruff, University of Michigan professor William Housel, a soil dynamics expert, William McLaughlin, the director of research and testing of the Michigan State Highway Department, and, of course, Berkey and Landes, who was included out of courtesy. As Woodfill had done earlier, Landes, although respected, was firmly put in his place. Early in the meeting, it was made clear that some thirty years previously Landes had been Berkey's student at the university. It was also made clear that Landes was not an engineer and Berkey was, and that geologists, especially Landes, should confine themselves to geological matters and recognize that it is the responsibility of engineers to provide solutions to problems even though they may be caused by geological formations. There was a great deal of discussion pro and con, aided by geological charts, profiles of soundings, and other data. The tension was dramatically relieved by Steinman pressing his thumb upon the two-inch oak tabletop around which we were all seated and saying, "The pressure of the proposed bridge foundations on the rock at the bottom of the Straits is equivalent to the pressure of my thumb on this table."

Although Landes's opinions were disproved by the experts, the press had already reported them and in order to finally and fully settle any disquiet about the rock at the bottom of the Straits, particularly as such doubt might affect the bond market, the Authority retained Housel and McLaughlin to make load-bearing tests at the Straits of Mackinac. They would actually build a platform in the Straits on material similar to that on which the bridge's foundations would rest and load it until the material crushed and became displaced.

A shallow hole was dredged down to rock near the shore, and the testing platform was built over it. Before the loading could be started, however, the Straits began to freeze. Housel and McLaughlin realized that if they could transport the load material, mostly rock, onto the platform over solid ice, it would be less costly than loading it onto a boat and then from the boat onto the platform. But to do this they would have to wait until the ice froze solid. There was some doubt about whether this delay would be permitted by the Authority. I was in Steinman's New York office when Housel phoned me about the problem. I told him that I would wire him a decision. After consulting with Steinman and Ammann, I decided that the delay would pose no problem. I sent Housel the wire: "Okay to delay load-bearing tests until hole freezes over."

Ultimately, the results of this empirical test revealed that the rock could bear four times the load that the proposed bridge foundations would place on it.

At the Authority meeting of April 27, 1951, it was revealed that Brown had met with Secretary of Defense Charles Wilson and other top federal officials and had been told that due to the Korean police action critical materials, such as steel, would not be available for the Mackinac Bridge until late 1952 or early 1953, barring an all-out war. Thus, it was decided to temporarily forego a request that the legislature pass a bill enabling the Authority to finance, build, and operate a bridge. It was also made clear at this meeting by State Highway Commissioner Ziegler that his department would assume responsibility neither for the cost of construction of bridge approaches nor for debt service.

However, at the next meeting of the Authority on September 13, 1951, Brown recommended that the legislature be requested to appropriate two to three million dollars (depending on engineers' estimates) from the Motor Vehicle Highway Fund for the preparation of final designs for the bridge. The fund would be reimbursed when the bonds were sold. Also, the legislature would be asked to pass the legislation to enable the Authority to sell the necessary bonds. None of these suggestions were officially acted upon at this meeting, although members were asked to make inquiries among design engineers regarding fees and to investigate the availability of steel from Canadian sources.

Several months later at an Authority meeting on January 22, 1952, it was moved by Osborn and seconded by Van Wagoner that the Authority "recommend to the Legislature a loan of $2,000,000 to be used for preparation of final designs, which loan would be repaid when the bridge is financed." It was deemed advisable to refrain from making a recommendation to the legislature as to the source of these funds. The motion carried unanimously. The Authority also drafted a plan for financing the rest of the bridge through the sale of bonds. What the minutes of this meeting did not reveal was that Highway Commissioner Ziegler was present and protecting his turf, the Motor Vehicle Highway Fund, and that the motion was made by a prominent Republican newspaper publisher, George Osborn, and seconded by Pat Van Wagoner, a former Democratic governor and highway commissioner. But this was about as political as the Authority ever got.

The recommendations were presented to the legislature, and, politics or not, the proposed legislation with the $2,000,000 appropriation got buried deeper in committee than the bridge foundations would eventually be in the Straits. Recognizing the realpolitik of the situation, the legislature reduced the appropriation to one dollar—for administrative purposes only. Otherwise, the appropriation would have disappeared entirely.

Then, the Authority brought in its engineers to address a joint session of the legislature. They made a good impression, as did Chairman Brown. The consulting traffic engineers also sent one of their partners to testify at a hearing of the Senate Appropriations Committee. After the hearing, the bill was sent to the floor of the Senate where it was debated for two days. During this discussion, it was stripped of any language even suggesting that the Highway Department or any other state agency might possibly pick up some of the bridge's costs, whether they be for construction, operation, maintenance, or debt service. Having been so amended, the bill passed the senate by a vote of twenty-six to one. Several days later it was adopted by the house in a vote of seventy to one and given immediate effect.

So the Authority had a hunting license: permission to sell revenue bonds to build the bridge, which, in turn, was expected to take in enough tolls to cover the cost of bridge operation, maintenance, and repair as well as repay the bond purchasers their interest and principal over the next forty years. Even if this were possible, as Coverdale & Colpitts maintained, there remained the nagging question, "Why, if this is such a good deal, doesn't the state or one of its agencies invest in it?" Brown and Fisher had already been asked this by some of their good friends in high financial circles. It would, however, serve no good purpose to answer or publicize it.

6

Van Ingen Is Confident

The legislation enabling the Authority to finance, build, and operate a bridge had passed. Designated Public Act 214 of the Public Acts of 1952, it was among a variety of newly enacted laws that had been cleared by the governor's legal advisor, printed, and routinely signed on April 30, 1952. There was no bill-signing ceremony in the governor's office.

Act 214, eight pages of legislative legalese containing twenty-one sections of fine print, empowered the Authority to issue revenue bonds "for the purpose of paying for the cost of a bridge." The remaining language consisted largely of limitations on the Authority for the protection of Michigan taxpayers and bondholders. At that time it did not seem important. Later, every clause, word, and punctuation mark had an impact.

The Authority now had the power to raise whatever funds were required to build the Mackinac Bridge. The money was to come from the sale of revenue bonds, which meant that the buyers of the bonds could depend only on the revenues of the bridge for a return on their investment.

What the legislation in effect said was, "Look, you

people want a bridge across the Straits of Mackinac. Okay, go ahead. Finance it and build it. But you cannot have the use of state funds for any part of it." And the lawmakers demonstrated their attitude toward the project by including the following sentence in section three of the act: "There is hereby appropriated from state highway funds the sum of one dollar to the authority which appropriation may be used to pay the cost of the organization of the authority and other preliminary costs incident thereto, and the planning of the bridge and the issuance of the bonds." Not a cent was allowed for engineering plans or construction.

Fairness requires an explanation of the one-dollar appropriation. It was included to overcome a procedural technicality. The legislature sets a deadline by which time all bills must clear the house or senate depending upon where they originate. If they do not meet the deadline, they are dead for the current legislative session. The exception to this rule is an appropriation measure. Since the bridge legislation was not approved before the deadline date set by the House of Representatives, where it was introduced, it was made an appropriation measure by including the one-dollar grant. However, it was always interesting to watch the reaction of persons who were told that the Authority was given a hunting license and one dollar to build a $100,000,000 bridge.

And the hunt would not be an easy one. Estimates of the cost of construction had been agreed upon and provided by the nation's three leading bridge designers. The country's foremost traffic consultants assured the Authority that the revenues of the bridge would be sufficient to repay the principal and interest on bonds sold to provide construction funds. A renowned engineering geologist, fortified with a load-bearing test, laid to rest any fears about the solidity of the rock formations on which the bridge piers would be founded. What more could the bankers want? Well, we were soon to find out—the hard way.

The Authority members were confident that with the enabling legislation passed the investment bankers would rush to underwrite the project. Toll roads and bridges all over the country were being financed through the sale of revenue bonds. But the bankers did not clamor to buy Mackinac Bridge bonds. Chairman Brown decided to call upon the Reconstruction Finance Corporation (RFC), a government agency created during the Great Depression, to help finance projects that could not quite make it in the private sector. He, along with Governor Williams, was cordially received in Washington. After all, Prentiss M. Brown had been a distinguished member of the Senate. The documentation for the project was submitted: the consulting engineers' report, the traffic consultants' report, the geologists' analysis, and even the optimistic conclusions of the Ebasco Report, a survey conducted by a private firm that specialized in economic analyses and forecasts, which predicted a bright future for Michigan's Upper Peninsula.

Undoubtedly the RFC pored through these papers, and one of its experts, Major A. W. Greeley (a descendant of "go-west" Horace Greeley), was dispatched to the Straits of Mackinac to make an on-site survey of the area. Naturally, Woodfill put him and his wife up at the Grand Hotel and acted as his host. The Greeleys were a little embarrassed by Woodfill's hospitality and reluctant to accept his complimentary profferings. But they did, and the weather cooperated; the scenery was magnificent; the accommodations were commodious; and the conclusion was disastrous. The RFC would not grant the Authority a loan. The agency, created before the New Deal, was phasing out its operations, having fulfilled the purpose for which it was created. Officially, all pending applications were to be cleared up and no new loans granted unless the project were "immediately urgent to the welfare of the community." The bridge, they deemed, was not.

During the remainder of the summer, the Authority made me a full-time employee and explored several other ideas for getting the project under way. One underwriter resurrected the 1941 plan to move the northern ferry terminal from its existing location in downtown St. Ignace several miles west to the end of the causeway that had been built for the bridge proposed in 1941. The Authority would be made responsible for the ferry service. The alleged savings of the shorter ferry trip would accrue to the Authority to provide seed money for future bridge financing. In the meantime the St. Ignace downtown merchants would lose the traffic upon which their existence depended; it would be necessary to construct a connecting highway that would cost hundreds of thousands of dollars, which would come from the state highway fund under the control of a commissioner who was dead set against the entire project; and the causeway would have to be raised to an elevation compatible with the loading and unloading ramps of the five ferry boats. But the material on which the causeway was built was adjudged so soft that it would be displaced like paste out of a tube if too much weight were placed on it.

One man, however, did come through with a feasible plan in the autumn of 1952. Brown received a letter from Bernard J. Van Ingen requesting an interview. Van Ingen was an investment banker and underwriter doing business under his own name and with a Wall Street address. We met with him in Detroit on October 17, 1952. He expressed confidence in his ability to put together a syndicate that would purchase our bonds. He had pioneered in the revenue bond financing of the Pennsylvania Turnpike prior to World War II and more recently had led the underwriting of the Ohio Turnpike to the tune of $326,000,000 in revenue bonds.

Van Ingen, tall, slim, and meticulously attired, was in his sixties. He spoke with a slight difficulty that possibly betrayed his recovery from a stroke. He exuded confidence in a quiet way—a way that appealed to the conservative Brown and Fisher. Thus it was that Van Ingen and Company became the Authority's underwriter of record.

There was much to be done. A consulting engineer would have to be retained to prepare construction plans so that firm bids could be obtained—estimates were not enough. After all, the Authority had to know with a fair degree of accuracy how many dollars it would take to build a bridge before borrowing the money (that is, selling the bonds). Then, the traffic report would have to be updated. If financing were to be carried out in early 1953, a traffic analysis based on 1950 figures would be obsolete, especially since ferry crossings had increased in the intervening years. Bond counselors would have to be retained. These are the attorneys whose opinions are necessary to assure prospective bond buyers that the project in which they are investing is what it purports to be. These opinions do not come cheap. Nor do the documents that must be published, the most important of which is the prospectus, known among financiers as the "red herring."

The red herring encapsulates all of the information available about the project: engineers' reports, traffic predictions, economic potential, insurance availability, reputation of the owners (in this case the Authority members), legal opinions as to the validity of the bond offering, tax effects, and whatever other pertinent information is necessary to assure the purchaser that he is making a sound investment.

Of course the Authority had no money to pay for all these additional services, but that did not seem to bother Van Ingen too much. He was confident that the attorneys would continue working on a contingency basis, as they had been doing since 1950. He would take care of the printing of documents, mailings, meetings, and other such matters connected with the syndication of the bonds. He did, however, advise the Authority to select a consulting engineer as soon as possible so that plans could be drawn and bids could be obtained before the proposed sale of the bonds in April. He was confident that the consulting engineer would work on the same contingency basis as the attorneys and the traffic people.

Chairman Brown asked the Authority engineering committee, now composed of members Van Wagoner, Ziegler, and Bricker, who replaced the deceased Zeder, to screen consulting engineers and make a recommendation to the Authority. It was decided that only the three consulting firms which had participated in the original feasibility study would be invited to make presentations. It should be recalled that the initial bridge legislation stated that the engineers who advised on feasibility would, as a protective measure, be prohibited from ultimately becoming the design consultants. But the Authority was so impressed with the integrity and the ability of the three men that they decided it would be unwise not to take advantage of their talents and experience for the final design responsibilities. The Authority could now do this because the enabling bond legislation removed the prohibition.

It was further decided that there would be no need for these men to go to the expense and inconvenience of coming to Detroit to attend the committee meeting which would take place on October 20, 1952. They were asked to submit presentations covering their backgrounds, staff organization, their willingness and ability to handle the project at this time, and most important, their expected fee. The material was to be in my hands by the appointed date of the meeting. Steinman called to ask my advice as to whether or not he should attend the meeting and make his presentation in person. I advised him not to attend. The committee members were well acquainted with all three consultants and had met with them in person many times. All they wanted now was an idea of organizational talent, accomplishments, time schedule, and fee. All this could be done with a written presentation. Because neither Ammann nor Woodruff had called to indicate that they wanted to attend, I advised Steinman that it would be unbecoming if he were the only one of the three to show up at the meeting. I was wrong. Ammann and Woodruff came, and the committee members were too polite not to receive them even though Steinman was left out. In retrospect, it probably helped him.

Woodruff spoke first. The odds were stacked against him. His credentials were first-class: he played an important role in the design of the great Oakland Bay Bridge and many other large structures in and around San Francisco. At that time, however, he did not have his own design firm and staff, although he did have a working arrangement with a large engineering-construction firm based in San Francisco.

It did not take long for Ammann to point out this weakness in Woodruff's presentation. I will never forget Ammann's rather harsh evaluation of Woodruff's capabilities. Nor was he kind to Steinman, pejoratively referring to Steinman's models of bridge sections—which he used to demonstrate the bridge's response to wind action—as toys. I shudder to think of what would have happened had Steinman been there.

Notwithstanding, two members of the committee were impressed with Ammann. The third member, Van Wagoner, was holding out for another firm which, during his administrations as highway commissioner and governor, had been responsible for the design of the Blue Water International Bridge between Michigan and Ontario. It goes without saying that Ziegler opposed this recommendation.

Ammann's reputation was impeccable. He had a substantial staff and had designed scores of important structures—the George Washington Bridge, the Whitestone, and many others in New York, throughout the United States, and abroad. He was an internationally famous bridge designer, and he wanted $1.25 million up front.

All three designers, in fact, wanted something up front. All three agreed to roughly the same percentage of the construction cost as their fee. So after a long afternoon, it was agreed by at least two members that they would recommend that Ammann be retained.

While Steinman was favorably regarded by all members of the committee, they felt he "advertised too much." At that time Steinman had a clipping service working for him and every item written about him, whether it appeared in *Engineering News-Record* or in a rural weekly, whether it was a brilliant dissertation on bridge design or a ten-line poem (poetry was an avocation of his), he would have about six hundred copies reproduced on glossy paper and mailed to friends he thought would be interested. I believe that this practice operated against him when he was being considered by the committee.

In due course the committee's recommendation of Ammann was relayed to Van Ingen with the understanding that the Authority could not provide the up-front money. It would be impossible to get it from the legislature, and State Highway Commissioner Ziegler certainly would not release any of his funds for the bridge.

Thus, it was up to Van Ingen to raise the money. He was reasonably confident that he could persuade Ammann to reconsider; or, failing that, he could prevail upon one of the big construction firms to advance the money. No one knows to this day what the quid pro quo would have been for such a loan, if it can be called that, but it was not all that unusual in helping to get a big construction project off the ground. Nevertheless, Van Ingen, despite his arduous efforts, had no success in raising money from contractors, nor did he succeed in persuading Ammann to work on a contingency basis. Van Ingen could not make the advance, so the Authority had no money for the plans. The project was stalemated.

About this time, in early October 1952, the American Bridge Tunnel and Turnpike Association was holding its annual convention in Detroit. I attended it, and I am sure it was no accident that I was befriended by Herbert Goodkind. Goodkind represented Steinman. Such an employee would normally be known as a marketing specialist, but to me he was a salesman—and a damned good one. He never pushed too much; he was knowledgeable, friendly, and outgoing; and he had an amazing capacity to drink whiskey all night and to be clearheaded early the next morning. He managed to sit next to me at association meals. He was always accompanied by his attractive wife and in his soft-sell manner let me know what a great engineer his boss was and how well-staffed his firm was. This often went on into the night.

Meanwhile, Van Ingen had made arrangements to invite the financial officers of seven or eight of the nation's top insurance companies to a gathering in Mackinaw City, the southern terminus of the proposed bridge, to observe Straits traffic for several days before the opening of Michigan's big-game (deer and bear) hunting season. The guests were the executives who advised their companies on bond purchases.

The Upper Peninsula was considered the happy hunting grounds, and the nimrods seeking passage from the Lower to the Upper Peninsula had often lined up for miles, as many as twenty-eight, and had waited for hours, as many as twenty-four, to get aboard one of the five ferry boats then in service. It was a rather dramatic annual ritual that always made headlines and drew columns of newspaper copy.

Once these financial officers—who decided on a daily basis where to invest the billions of dollars of premiums flowing into insurance company coffers—saw this lineup of traffic they would realize the need for a permanent connecting link and would presumably be ready to buy when the bonds were offered. Without their support, the sale of the bonds would go poorly. They were the "bell cows" of the revenue bond financing business.

Well, Goodkind and I got onto the subject of deer hunting, and since I had a cabin in the Lower Peninsula that was the annual gathering place of some hearty imbibers, I invited him to be my guest for the opening of the season on November 15, 1952. And I added that he might as well come to the Straits of Mackinac and view the hunting traffic. When I extended this invitation early in October, prior to the engineering committee meeting, his firm was still being considered as a possible designing consultant.

Duncan Grey, Van Ingen's right-hand man, arrived in my office in Lansing on November 11, 1952. Another member of Van Ingen's firm had been in Mackinaw City making arrangements for the insurance executives scheduled to arrive the next morning. Grey, in his early thirties, was smart beyond his years. From an office boy and runner, he had risen in the firm to become a vice-president and the boss's chief assistant. Small, prematurely gray, and in possession of a keen sense of humor, he quickly won the respect of the Authority members who dealt with him.

Grey was worried. He outlined the problems with which we were all confronted. His boss had not had any luck with Ammann or with the contractors, and he simply did not know where to get the up-front money for bidding plans. It was now three weeks since the engineering committee had decided on Ammann and about five weeks since I had met Goodkind in Detroit at the convention and had invited him to my hunting cabin. I had forgotten the invitation until that very moment when Goodkind walked into my office while Grey and I were bemoaning our hard luck.

He planted his 250-pound frame on one of the chairs near my desk after being introduced to Grey. I was a bit surprised to see him—I had long assumed that he had heard about the committee's preference for Ammann and had bowed out. Usually that sort of news gets around quickly, although the Authority had not publicized it because Ammann's selection had not yet been officially confirmed by the Authority.

My own surprise was eclipsed by Goodkind's shock when I broke the news. His superficial calm and self-control were superb. He even managed not to bite the most closely bitten fingernails I have ever seen. His insides were no doubt roiling and broiling, but he had the perseverance to inquire whether or not the decision was final. Duncan Grey pointed out that efforts to get Ammann to forego his up-front money had not been successful.

This was all Goodkind needed. He immediately started to negotiate with Grey. It seemed to me at the time that as secretary of the Authority I had better not be a party to these negotiations. Although it was Armistice Day, a legal holiday, a phone call to my friend C. J. ("Irish") Carroll, director of the Michigan Road Builders' Association, revealed that he was in his office and would gladly make a room and telephone available for Grey and Goodkind.

So off they went to the Road Builders' office in the Michigan National Bank Building. And negotiate they did.

They related their activities to me while driving to the Straits that afternoon. A certain amount of protocol had to be followed. First, Grey had called his boss to make sure that it was all right to discuss the matter with the Steinman firm. It was entirely possible that between the time that Grey left New York and the time he called that there could have been a development with Ammann. For example, Ammann could have relented a little on his demands, and, if so, the merest suspicion that Van Ingen might be negotiating elsewhere would have upset any progress with Ammann. He instructed Grey to discuss the matter with the Steinman people, but to make no commitment without approval from the Authority.

Goodkind then called his boss to find out if he were willing to prepare plans for bidding purposes with the understanding that he would be paid if and when the bonds were sold. It would be quite a gamble. His payroll would run into six figures and increase with each passing month until the Authority received the proceeds of the bond sale, if ever. In addition, there was the matter of his reputation: no consultant wants to be identified with a loser.

Steinman (who earned his doctorate before he was twenty years old and had already received honorary doctoral degrees from eighteen universities) had faith in the Mackinac Bridge project. He was willing to gamble. He told Goodkind to go ahead.

7

A Natural Disaster

The euphoria that accompanied our trip north proved to be ephemeral. We were going to help host the financial officers of the leading insurance companies invited by Van Ingen to the Straits to witness the dramatic backup of the thousands of deer hunters trying to reach the Upper Peninsula before the November 15 opening of the season. November weather at the Straits is usually windy, wet, and cold. The five ferry boats would battle the turbulent Straits, struggling to transport the impatient hunters. The latter would converge on Mackinaw City far more rapidly than the boats could carry them. It was not unusual for long lines of traffic to develop. Feature writers feasted on stories of hunter behavior under these trying conditions. Thus, the need for a permanent, all-weather link connecting Michigan's two peninsulas was widely dramatized in the press at least once a year. We wanted the financial officers to witness this need for a bridge first hand.

So what happened? From November 12 until the early morning hours of November 15, when the season would open at sunrise, the Straits was as calm as a millpond. The five ferry boats in service never transported vehicles with such speed and efficiency. None of the lineups developed along the highway. There were no battles among frustrated hunters trying to buck the line. None of the cars were gassed up with fifty-foot-long hoses as drivers refused to leave their places in the line. No bonfires were set on the road shoulders. There was none of the boisterous behavior that made great newspaper copy—and fodder for fireside hyperbole.

It all appeared so calm and routine that our visitors from New York probably thought that moving Straits traffic was nothing compared with the confrontations of the big city. To make matters worse we kept saying, "Just wait till tomorrow." Well, tomorrow came, but the lineups did not.

Van Ingen's associates, Bridge Authority people, and scores of Chamber of Commerce representatives from the Upper Peninsula provided the finest, friendliest, most gracious hospitality possible, but that was not the bottom line. The financial officers quickly perceived that the permanent population of Mackinaw City was nine hundred; and that St. Ignace was a metropolis of three thousand souls. This observation was underscored by a tour of the cities of Sault Ste. Marie, Michigan, and Sault Ste. Marie, Ontario, which were fifty miles north. They are located on opposite shores of the St. Mary's River, and an authority had already been established to finance and build a bridge connecting the two cities. These communities appeared by comparison far more attractive to the financiers. The American city had a trading area of about twenty thousand persons and the Canadian, sixty thousand. The Algomah Steel Mills, the Abitibi Pulp and Paper Company, and the immensely attractive Soo Locks were in full view of the prospective bond buyers as we cruised along the St. Mary's River on a lovely, warm, sunny day in November.

"Why don't you build a bridge up here?" asked several members of the party. What could we say?

If this were not enough, we were soon confronted with another crisis.

A farewell dinner was planned for the guests in Mackinaw City on the night of November 14. Early that day, State

Highway Commissioner Ziegler had arrived unexpectedly in Mackinaw City. The news that he was in town spread quickly. Many of our visitors were aware that the commissioner, as the state's foremost highway officer, was not enthusiastic about a Mackinac Straits bridge. He had recently built and pressed into service at the Straits a five-million-dollar, double-ended, ice-breaking ferryboat and had spent several million more to upgrade docking facilities.

Grey and I had to decide whether or not to invite Ziegler to the dinner. We carefully weighed the pros and cons. If he were invited, he would not only meet and talk with our guests but would also have to be asked to make a few remarks along with other speakers scheduled to review the entire event. And this was the man who once told me he could not supply me with a copy of the Highway Department's monthly ferry traffic figures because the typist could only make nine copies and their distribution was already determined! On the other hand, if he were not invited, it might appear that we were trying to hide something from our guests. Grey argued that the situation was tenuous enough and should not be made any shakier. We could not afford any further negative events or opinions. It was not an easy decision. After all, Ziegler was an ex-officio member of the Authority, and even though no other members were present, the Authority, and therefore Ziegler, were, in a manner of speaking, co-hosts.

My view, to my sorrow, prevailed. I had hoped that when I interrupted his card game the afternoon of the dinner to extend an invitation, Ziegler would beg off to keep another appointment somewhere along the 110,000 miles of highways, roads, and streets with which he should have been concerned. No such luck; he accepted with alacrity.

Poor Grey. I thought he would have a stroke. One after another of our guests cornered Ziegler during cocktails before dinner and got his personal and professional view of the bridge proposal. Those who missed it then certainly got it during his remarks after dinner.

He made his usual bridge speech introduction: he said

he was certainly in favor of the project, and then he launched into his laundry list of disclaimers which he had been raising since the creation of the Authority two years earlier. He spoke of the number of days that the wind at the Straits reached velocities of more than sixty miles per hour. He mentioned the windrows of ice that would pile up as high as forty feet where the foundations were planned. He was confident that the engineers, with "enough money," could design foundations that would not collapse the soft limestone underlying the Straits. It was a disaster!

Goodkind and the rest of us did all we could in the aftermath to refute these criticisms, pointing out that the obstacles Ziegler discussed had been anticipated and could be overcome. But it was too little and too late. Those insurance company vice-presidents returned to their home offices, closed the books on the Mackinac Bridge, and resumed their analyses of possible investments in Florida's Sunshine Skyway, the Maine Turnpike, and the Indiana Turnpike, bonds, all of which would be offered for sale in the near future.

Our venture was a dismal failure, but none of us would admit it. We were not involved in this project to be pessimistic. We realized that when the bonds were actually offered for sale, the decision makers would let the numbers do the talking, and they would ultimately take a hard look at the bottom line.

Not all the results of our efforts, however, were negative. The financiers were afforded an opportunity to get a favorable view of the proposed Sault International Bridge (across the St. Mary's River), and Goodkind salvaged something for his firm. He made the most of the opportunity to get acquainted with the members of the Sault Ste. Marie International Bridge Authority and before leaving the Straits area had pretty well sewed up an engineering consulting arrangement with that organization. Of course, that authority still had to sell bonds to get its project financed, but that's another story.

Undaunted, Van Ingen decided to proceed with the formation of an underwriting syndicate and sell the bonds. A great deal of groundwork was required. The prospectus had to be proofread for accuracy by all parties concerned: engineers, lawyers, the Authority, insurance brokers, traffic consultants, and geologists. Payout tables had to be prepared to show that the expected bridge revenues would be more than adequate to meet all the obligations: the cost of maintenance, operation, and repair; the payment of interest and principal; the cost of insurance; the accumulation of reserves; and, after all these demands were fulfilled, there would still have to be a cushion of 20 percent. It was a formidable requirement. Under the direction of the sharp-penciled Grey, though, the document was completed.

Also completed were arrangements for a grand presentation in the great hall of the New York State Board of Commerce, where about 225 representatives of the nation's leading bond brokers were to assemble on March 18, 1953. Governor Williams and Brown attended, and with legislative leaders and even Michigan's State Treasurer, D. Hale Brake, they sang the praises of the proposed bridge. The audience obviously was not tuned in. When Van Ingen later asked for commitments from those who attended the meeting, only about a third of the proposed $96,000,000 offering was spoken for. Van Ingen advised postponement and reasoned that the lukewarm response was caused by uncertain government policies, other competitive bond issues, and most of all the fact that the state of Michigan was not participating financially in the project.

He strongly recommended that the Authority remedy this last criticism by requesting the legislature to appropriate $500,000 toward bridge operation, maintenance, and repair. He pointed out very reasonably that the ferry service was losing about that much annually. Thus, the appropriation for maintenance would only be a substitution of the bridge for the ferry at no increased cost to the state. With that gesture he was confident the bonds could be sold.

Shortly thereafter, a bill was introduced to appropriate $500,000 annually out of the Motor Vehicle Highway Fund to the Mackinac Bridge Authority to offset the cost of operat-

ing, maintaining, and repairing the bridge. The appropriation would become effective when the bridge was opened to
traffic. Some clever legislator noted that Steinman's bridge
engineering report had estimated that during the first year
of operation, maintenance costs would be $416,900. The bill
was amended to reduce the original $500,000 appropriation
to $417,000.

8

Emil Peltz Saves the Day

It was war—war between Democratic Governor Williams and the Republican-dominated legislature. By mid-May 1953, it came down to a clear-cut issue: the passage of a business activities tax otherwise known as BAT. Pass BAT, said the legislative leadership, or all appropriations bills will be blocked—the onus of which would fall upon the governor. When payrolls are not met, bills unpaid, utilities threatening to discontinue service, it is much easier to lay the blame at the feet of one individual, the governor, rather than a number of lesser-known legislators. Thus, the latter could with impunity carry out their threat to bury all appropriations bills.

Notwithstanding the fact that there were more Republicans in the house than there were Democrats, the Republican leadership was not certain about the passage of BAT. Somehow there emerged from among its many articles, sections, subsections, and paragraphs the suspicion that BAT did not hurt the big corporations as much as it did small businesses. Many rural Republicans were fed up with the way big business and corporate lobbyists played up to some legislative leaders while taking the "hicks" for granted.

So on the cool, damp spring night of May 19, 1953, the

Republicans voted for a recess to caucus and count noses to determine whether or not there were enough votes to bring BAT to the floor. They needed fifty-one votes for passage, and while there were fifty-four Republicans in the house, not all would vote in favor of the legislation. The Democrats were disciplined, and none could be counted on to break ranks and vote for BAT. Thus, the BAT supporters had to get the votes out of the caucus. They were getting desperate because if they did not get those votes then they would have to carry out their threat to hold up all appropriations, an action that would bring Michigan's government to a standstill.

In retrospect I don't believe the legislature would actually have allowed that to happen, but at the time I wasn't so sure—nor was anyone else I knew around the capitol. In the eyes of the Republicans an upstart Democrat sat in the governor's chair, and in the eyes of the governor, Neanderthal Republicans dominated the legislature.

What has all this to do with the proposed Mackinac Bridge? Well, hidden somewhere among the appropriation bills that would keep mental institutions open, highways abuilding, schools operating, and police policing was a simple little measure that said $417,000 per year would be appropriated out of highway funds to the Mackinac Bridge Authority for the operation, maintenance, and repair of the bridge, if indeed it were ever built and opened for traffic. The legislation contained a time limit: if the structure were not financed by December 31, 1953, the appropriation would not carry over to 1954.

It was not a controversial measure. There were at least two disclaimers: it had to be successfully financed by the end of the year and its construction had to be completed. At least half the legislature did not think either could be accomplished, but it was an appropriation bill and as such was doomed to failure along with all other appropriation bills. Even delay could mean failure because the Authority had already awarded construction contracts for the substructure and superstructure, about 90 percent of the total bridge costs. Thus, the number of bonds to be sold was known. But these contracts were good only until June 30, 1953. After that, the contractors would be constrained to raise their prices due to inflation. No one was certain that the expected bridge revenues would cover the additional costs. From mid-May to the end of June was not much time when one considers all the steps that must be taken before proceeds of a revenue bond issue of the size contemplated are in hand. The outlook was dark. If BAT did not pass, the Mackinac Bridge would not be built.

Caucuses are supposed to be secret, but somehow some information gets out. Participants have to go to the bathroom, make phone calls, or break dates. When they step out of the caucus room they inevitably run into somebody who has an interest in what is going on "and can keep a secret."

One such person was Senator Leo Roy of Hancock, Michigan, home of Michigan Technological University (then Michigan College of Mining and Technology). The school was the senator's favorite project, and he had promised it a new hockey rink and building, which required passage of an appropriation bill.

Roy was also a supporter of the Mackinac Bridge. So when I spotted him in the gallery where I was awaiting the results of the caucus, I approached him to find out if he knew anything. The length of his face was a dead giveaway.

"Have you heard anything?" I asked.

"Yeah, they ain't got enough votes for BAT and my hockey rink and your bridge are going down the drain," he replied.

This only added to the misery of a spring allergy I was suffering from. My eyes were burning, my nose running, and I was chain sneezing, sometimes so violently that I thought my head would explode. I might as well go home. On the way out of the capitol I ran into the assistant to the most powerful lobbyist in Lansing. He had first-hand, late information about the caucus. He sympathized with my loss of the bridge bill.

Once back at the apartment I thought a hot shower would alleviate some of my misery. No sooner was I all soaped up than the chap with whom I shared quarters shouted that there was a phone call for me and that I should hurry. It was Emil Peltz.

Emil Peltz.

The name says little. But Peltz's hardware store in the small community of Rogers City in the northeast corner of Michigan's Lower Peninsula was well known, and well respected.

The potato and dairy farmers who traded there, and whose names revealed a European origin similar to Peltz, liked the cigar-chomping, silver-thatched merchant well enough to send him to Lansing as their Republican member of the House of Representatives.

Once there his character became apparent. He was sturdy, steady, and wise if not quick. He was not above accepting a drink, or even a bottle, from a lobbyist, but he was far above being bought. He was determined, if not stubborn, and principled, if not proud.

In due course he rose to the coveted position of chairman of the House Roads and Bridges Committee. For years the cities, counties, and State Highway Department vied with each other for a bigger share of motor vehicle taxes, which by constitutional guarantee at that time were earmarked for highway (state and U.S. trunklines), county road, and municipal street purposes only.

Representative Peltz was instrumental in knocking a few figurative heads together. He was fed up with the bickering and backbiting by the aforementioned governmental agencies and their satellite supporters as they lobbied legislators from dawn to dusk, and many from dusk to dawn, each trying to get the biggest share of the motor vehicle fund for his or her constituency.

About this time the Automotive Safety Foundation, headquartered in Washington, D.C., had completed a scientific study of Michigan's highway needs. Peltz was influential in getting the three competing government agencies to agree to abide by the results of the study. Thus, the job of the chairman of the House Roads and Bridges Committee and its members would become considerably less complicated.

The Michigan Good Roads federation, an association of public and private organizations and individuals dedicated to highway improvement, had retained the Automotive Safety Foundation to make the study. The federation then hired me for two months to publicize the results in order to obtain grassroots support for the legislative changes recommended. They were embodied in seven separate proposals which, after introduction in the legislature, were sent to the House Roads and Bridges Committee. That is how I met Emil Peltz.

For reasons unimportant to this narrative the legislation did not pass. However, my eight-week assignment was extended to four years, during which time I had many opportunities to get well acquainted with Peltz. By the middle of 1950 I was wearing two hats: executive director of the Michigan Good Roads Federation and secretary of the Mackinac Bridge Authority.

One spring afternoon, an overcast, bone-chilling day, we were driving from Lansing to Grand Rapids to attend the annual banquet of the Michigan Good Roads Federation. A lull in the conversation was broken by Peltz's question.

"Tell me, Larry, what's the scoop on this bill to enable the Mackinac Bridge Authority to borrow money to build the bridge? Is it legit or are you going to stick the state general fund or the motor vehicle fund to pay for it?"

We spent the next hour going over all facets of the bridge-enabling legislation, the traffic studies and predictions, the estimates of the consulting engineers, the rebuttals to the critics of the proposed structure. By the time we arrived in Grand Rapids Peltz knew more about the Mackinac Bridge, its proposed financing, construction, operation, and maintenance, than any other member of the legislature.

Strangely, this was not a lobbying event. His committee had already reported the legislation favorably and at no particular risk, since it was only an enabling act permitting the

Authority to search for somebody to underwrite the sale of about $100,000,000 of revenue bonds.

What I did not know was that about a year later our discussion would bear fruit—fruit so important that without it there very likely would not have been a Mackinac Bridge. But I was not thinking of this as I rinsed off and grabbed a towel on my way to the phone. What would Peltz want at this hour? I picked up the telephone.

"Hey, where were you? I looked all over the gallery and there was no sign of you."

"Well, I heard you fellows couldn't get enough votes for BAT and that you were going to hang tough on appropriation bills, so I went home," I replied.

"Yeh, that's right, too bad you missed it," he said.

"Missed what?"

"Missed the passage of your bill, you idiot," he replied.

"Aw, c'mon, Emil, I feel lousy enough as it is without your needling me."

"I'm not needling you. Now listen to me. You get a bottle of booze and get your ass up to Room 611 pronto. We're going to celebrate."

"Emil are you serious? What happened?" I demanded.

"Never mind now, you get down here and I'll tell you all about it."

It was about 10:30 P.M. I scrounged around and luckily found an unopened bottle. I stuffed it into my pocket and drove to the Olds Hotel some three miles away. I still was not sure what had happened and was not quite ready to celebrate. I had witnessed some of Representative Peltz's practical jokes before and was apprehensive about being the butt of one now.

However, my spirits were buoyed a bit when during the ride up the elevator I ran into the house minority leader, who looked at me and said in a tone which I thought was laced with bitterness or jealousy, "Well, you got what you wanted." I said nothing.

When I entered Room 611 Peltz greeted me with a great

big bear hug—even before I produced the bottle.

"Well, we beat the bastards, we really did. We rubbed their noses in dirt," he cried.

"Emil, what in hell are you talking about?" I could not understand his rapture over the passage of the bridge bill, if indeed that was what he was bellowing about. It was of very little political value to him. His voting district was in the northeastern part of the Lower Peninsula, and among many short-sighted, small-minded persons, a bridge making the recreational attractions of the Upper Peninsula more accessible could spell less tourist business in his jurisdiction. Of course, it didn't turn out that way.

"What happened?" I repeated as I poured a drink for him and several others in the room.

He sat down, leaned back, and savored his drink almost as much as what he related.

The caucus leaders counted noses for BAT support and came up a couple of votes short. They made a few speeches. They tried some buttonholing, lapel tugging, and even arm twisting, but still fifty-one votes did not materialize.

Just when it looked like the caucus would break up, Peltz asked to be heard. Up to this point no one had paid much attention to him or to any of the other upstate people.

"I'll vote for BAT and guarantee you three more votes if you'll suspend the rules and move the bridge legislation off the docket and onto the floor for immediate passage," he announced.

There was a brief silence while the leadership tried to comprehend the impact of the deal and determine whether or not it had any hidden curves.

It did. It said, "You guys have been ignoring us, taking us for granted, and now we want our due. You're going to do it our way. You want BAT. We want recognition and the way we will get it is for you to pass the Mackinac Bridge appropriation first!"

And that is exactly what the legislature did.

With the passage of the $417,000 appropriation, our prospects of successful financing skyrocketed. Even Woodfill was delighted to hail Peltz's and my efforts as heroic. He had been asked by Brown to cut short his Colorado vacation and come to Lansing to rescue the appropriation bill, which at the moment was still in committee. He requested a meeting with me upon his arrival to bring him up to date. In effect, I told him that I did not think there was much he could do, that I thought I had the matter well in hand (this was before the BAT versus appropriations strategy). He then suggested that he might catch the next train back to Colorado, and I agreed.

So Van Ingen went back to planning another bond offering for early June, but as luck would have it, he suffered a severe heart attack in the interim. His firm was in the throes of determining leadership and advised the Authority that the planned June offering would have to be delayed. This was a blow to the Authority. Contingency contract dates passed; prospects for financing a bridge were indeed dim.

A New Pitch

During the summer of 1953, everything concerned with the bridge seemed to be at a standstill. Nothing was accomplished—at least so far as the Authority could see. Yet, in retrospect, there were some very important activities going on, many of which the members of the Authority were not privy to. Newspapers were alluding to the Wall Street "summer doldrums," but those financiers who may have vacationed away from downtown New York did not ignore opportunities when they saw them.

For example, a man by the name of Stuart Silloway, financial vice-president of the Mutual Life of New York Insurance Company, was making an extended tour of northern Michigan. He was impressed. Early in October, he called on Authority vice-chairman Fisher and conveyed his optimism, if not enthusiasm, about the prospects of a Straits crossing.

He suggested, however, that the Authority adopt the financing strategy employed by the New Jersey Turnpike Authority. It was called the "drawdown-forward commitment." It is a financing procedure wherein the borrower (the Authority) receives funds from the lenders (the bond purchasers) only in amounts necessary to pay contractors as they complete portions of their work. The advantage of this procedure is that the borrower does not pay interest on the full amount of the funds necessary to complete the entire project.

For example, if the entire cost of the Mackinac Bridge were to be $100,000,000, the interest rate at the time 4 percent, and the construction period four years, then the Authority would have to pay $4,000,000 in interest for four years, or $16,000,000 before earning one cent of revenue.

But with the drawdown-forward commitment plan, the Authority would only pay interest on the amount borrowed to pay the contractors for the amount of work they had completed. Assuming the work progressed at an equal rate of 25 percent for each of the four construction years, the Authority would borrow $25,000,000 the first year. At 4 percent, the interest cost for that year would be only $1,000,000 instead of $4,000,000. The second year's interest cost would be $2,000,000, the third, $3,000,000, and the fourth, $4,000,000, for a total of $10,000,000 in interest costs instead of $16,000,000 when all the money is received at the outset.*

The idea sounded most encouraging to Brown and Fisher, so they packed their bags and went to Wall Street and its environs to sound out insurance company executives. They met with officers of Prudential, Mutual, Equitable, New York Life, Sun Life, and Metropolitan. The responses were about even between "definite interest" and ."unfavorable."

Perhaps a bit carried away by Silloway's encouragement, or possibly because they were men accustomed to overcoming technical obstacles, they had not consulted with legal counsel regarding the use of the drawdown-forward procedure. Had they done so, John Nunneley, the Authority's legal counsel, would have told them that "unless the most

---

*This example oversimplifies the arithmetic. In actual practice, the Authority would be able to invest the proceeds of a bond issue that were not used for construction. The savings normally would be less than the $6,000,000 shown in the example.

reliable and financially solid insurance companies in the country would participate in the drawdown-forward commitment plan, the practicality of such a procedure would be difficult, if not impossible, from a legal point of view."

He explained that there was a requirement in the enabling legislation that the Authority offer its bonds for sale to the public. He added that insurance companies generally do not bid in public competition, but prefer to negotiate. "How can you be sure that the companies participating in the drawdown would have the funds available at some future date? If they don't, the Authority will be left with a part of the bridge and no money," he warned.

So much for the drawdown-forward commitment plan. At about the same time Silloway was expressing positive ideas to Fisher, another conversation concerning the proposed Mackinac Bridge took place in New York. In fact, it took place at Yankee Stadium during the third game of the World Series between the New York Yankees and the Brooklyn Dodgers.

Two executives in box seats were discussing the proposed financing of a bridge in northern Michigan. One was the rotund, florid-faced, and cherubic James S. Abrams, Jr., of Allen & Company, the Wall Street investment bankers. The other was his guest, Fred Lowe, assistant vice-president and financial analyst of the New York Life Insurance Company. He was a dour, thin-lipped man with an overall undernourished appearance.

"Jim," said Fred, "have you looked at that Mackinac Bridge proposition?"

"No, Van Ingen has an underwriting agreement with the Authority and it wouldn't be right to stick my nose in it."

"I don't think Van Ingen is interested anymore," said Lowe. "The old man has been sick. Jim Couffer and Walter Dempsey [B. J. Van Ingen & Company vice-presidents] are not keen about bond underwriting right now. I've been studying the engineering and traffic reports. If we can get a preferred position on the bonds we might be interested in a sizeable investment."

Abrams took another bite of his ball park hotdog and another swig of beer; the wheels of his ever-fertile brain were spinning rapidly. But just then a sensational catch brought the people in the stands to their feet applauding and buzzing about the game-saving effort.

Later that day, the two baseball fans resumed their bridge discussion at the men's bar of the Plaza Hotel. By dinner time, Abrams had already formulated a plan and procedure.

First, he would get a release from the Van Ingen firm; then he would ask for a meeting with the Authority; and third, he would fortify himself with a good-faith check for $500,000, and, when he met with the Authority or its officers, he would make them a proposition they could not refuse: he would offer to buy the entire $100,000,000 bond issue. With New York Life willing to buy a large block of bonds in return for a prior lien—at a slight discount—Abrams was confident he could handle the entire issue.

Whether or not Abrams dreamed that night of a five-mile-long bridge spanning the turbulent Straits of Mackinac in northern Michigan only he would remember. But now history should record that the relatively short and interrupted conversation during and following a World Series baseball game may have sparked the flame that ultimately resulted in the construction of the Mackinac Bridge. It would be inaccurate to permit the impression that from that moment on all went swimmingly. In fact, the opposite was true.

10

Jim Abrams's Offer

It was Armistice Day—not the first Monday of the month but the original, traditional eleventh hour of the eleventh day of the eleventh month.

This Armistice Day of 1953 was only about fifty days before the expiration of the legislation granting $417,000 annually for bridge operation, maintenance, and repair, if and when it were ever opened for traffic. If the bonds to finance the construction were not sold by December 31, 1953, the legislation would expire and the grant would be withdrawn.

Realistically, the chances for financing before the end of the year were few, if any. With less than two months remaining, no underwriter or financial institution had indicated even a general interest. Only persons of great faith and a never-say-die character would hold any hope. Only eternal optimists such as Brown, Fisher, and I were still pursuing the elusive "bell cow" that would lead investors and underwriters into the corral of Mackinac Bridge bond purchasers.

The object was to persuade the finance committee or board of directors of a leading financial institution, such as a large insurance company, a national bank, or even one of the big brokerage houses, to buy a substantial block of the bonds, perhaps $10,000,000 worth. Such a commitment would start the ball rolling and other investors would follow. Brown and Fisher were taking full advantage of their Wall Street connections and had appointments with the presidents of several large insurance companies and banks that week of November 8, 1953.

About ten days earlier Brown had received a letter from James Abrams. Because Allen & Company was not among the so-called Big Seventeen, Brown was not too enthusiastic about Abrams's request to meet with him to discuss a bond underwriting idea which, Abrams said in his letter, he was certain would result in the successful financing of the bridge.

It should be pointed out that during the late forties and early fifties there was a plethora of revenue bond financing. Toll roads, bridges, dormitories, and a host of other projects that should have been built during World War II were in demand. To finance and build them on a cash basis would have required the levying of huge tax increases. Borrowing was more practical and palatable. Public agencies or authorities were created and empowered by legislation to do the borrowing and building. The agencies would sell bonds, and the interest paid to buyers would be exempt from federal income taxes. Both the principal and the interest would be paid back from tolls or revenues generated by the projects.

Most of the underwriting of these projects was carried out by the Big Seventeen. These seventeen firms seemed to have a strong grip on bond offerings and could readily form a syndicate that would guarantee their sale. Actually, there were fewer than seventeen that seemed to get the best and biggest deals, but the number somehow gained wide circulation and recognition in the financial world.

Allen & Company, although recently successful in some powerful financial feats, such as taking over the Colorado Fuel and Iron Company, was not considered big league. But November 11, 1953, was a bank holiday and Brown and Fisher had only one afternoon appointment with an insurance company president. So they decided, and I was to join them, to give Abrams an audience that morning.

The meeting began at 10 A.M. in the National Bank of Detroit suite on the ninth floor of the Drake Hotel in New York. Abrams's white hair crowned a face enlivened by quick, blue eyes that could be smiling or cold as steel depending upon the tenor of the conversation. During the initial small talk he let it be known that he had given up his fox hunting that morning. Frankly, I was not impressed and, after sizing up his physique, a bit doubtful. If Brown or Fisher were impressed I don't know and it really did not make any difference. As soon as Abrams got serious, he had something to say.

"Gentlemen, I'm confident that Allen & Company can underwrite your bonds, and we are prepared to go forward at once with the financing." These were the boldest and most optimistic words we had heard since our first meeting with Van Ingen thirteen months earlier.

"You're quite confident, Mr. Abrams," said Brown, "that you can really underwrite these bonds and outbid the larger Wall Street firms in a public sale?"

"A public sale?" repeated Abrams, hesitating for a moment. He was under the impression that the sale of the bonds could be negotiated. In fact, he had a check for $500,000 in his pocket and fully intended to close the deal that day.* Notwithstanding this turn of events, the resourceful Abrams came up with a plan.

"Yes, I'm sure we can manage it. If I may say so, I think you people are trying to sell too many bonds at one time, especially for a project in such an isolated area."

---

*I, of course, did not know about the $500,000 check because it never came up at that November 11, 1953, meeting. Not until twenty-nine years later, when Abrams was attending the twenty-fifth anniversary of the bridge opening on November 1, 1982, did he mention it while reminiscing about the meeting.

"I nearly fell through the floor," he related, "but I managed to maintain my cool because I was convinced it was a good deal and, public sale or not, we could handle it."

I chided him about not doing his homework. He should have known a public offering was required. He countered, somewhat sheepishly, that most of the recent legislation creating and empowering authorities to sell bonds permitted negotiated sales, and he assumed this was true of Mackinac. Even experts have difficulty with the fine print.

I was tempted to ask him what else was new and was glad I did not because, as it turned out, it was the preface to the most important recommendation any financier ever made to the Mackinac Bridge Authority.

"What I would like to suggest is that you break your issue into two parts: say eighty million with a first lien* on revenues, and twenty million with a second lien, but with a little higher interest rate.

"That would give your first lien bonds better coverage† than you were able to show on your previous efforts to finance, while the second lien bonds, because of their higher interest rate, would be more attractive to investors who are not so concerned about risk."

"Who," inquired Fisher, "would be willing to buy the second lien bonds?"

We had been having a hell of a time trying to sell any bonds let alone those with a second-place rating.

"Michigan has several funds that invest in bonds all the time. There is the Teachers Retirement Fund, the Veterans Fund. I think these bonds would be attractive to the fund managers since they would support a Michigan project—for the good of the state," he replied.

Good grief, I thought, here we are back to square one. Sure the Mackinac Bridge was a Michigan project and aside from a few conservatives, diehards, politicians, and professional doubters, everybody was for a bridge—providing it was built at no risk to him or her.

At that time I think the World War II veterans would have rearmed and stormed the capitol if any of their funds had been used to buy Mackinac Bridge bonds, and the teachers would have risen in righteous wrath if their sacred retire-

---

*First, or Series A, lien bonds means that the holders of these bonds have first claim on any funds available for payment of interest and principal, while the second lien, or Series B, bond holders get their interest after the semiannual payments are made of A bonds and are redeemed only after all the A bonds are redeemed.

†Coverage refers to how much the revenues of the project exceed all expenses and obligations of interest payments and commitments to the sinking fund and reserves. Mackinac Bridge financing was predicated on 1.20 coverage.

ment funds were invested in a project with questionable predicted earnings.

"If you're depending upon Michigan funds to buy the B bonds then I think there's no point in any further discussion," I said.

"That's no problem," he replied with smiling confidence. "I'm quite certain those twenty million second lien bonds can be placed. In fact, Charles Allen, the chairman of our company, might buy them himself."

Withholding an expletive, I thought to myself that this guy must either be a charlatan, an optimist, or the world's greatest financier. Yet there was something about him that exuded confidence and a let's-do-it attitude. Even when confronted with the fact that the financing had to be completed before December 31, he reflected for a moment, and in a firm voice that carried the utmost conviction said, "It can be done."

I do not want to give readers the impression that the preceding took place in the one-two-three fashion described above. The quotes are reasonably accurate, but there was a drawn-out discussion among Abrams, Brown, Fisher, and myself. In fact, it continued through lunch, with the understanding that Abrams would submit his proposal in writing for consideration by the entire Authority. We in turn would consult with attorneys, local bankers, and bond experts. He agreed to make his presentation to the Authority's Executive Committee in Detroit on November 17, 1953.

Abrams turned out to be a rather pleasant person, jolly, always ready with a chuckle, yet firm and direct when necessary. Throughout the discussion, he answered all our questions reasonably. Attempting to assure ourselves that his firm had the capability of handling our bond issue, we had to ask penetrating and perhaps embarrassing questions. This did not faze him. Sometimes, his eyes narrowed a bit, but he always maintained his pleasant mien, his firm self-control and air of confidence. By the time lunch was over, I personally felt we were really going to beat that year-end deadline.

While finishing my coffee at lunch, though, my mind wandered at bit and I visualized Abrams as a New Amsterdam burgher circa 1660. He would be a natural sitting in front of a roaring fireplace, dressed in pantaloons, brocade vest, and loose white shirt, and puffing on a long-stemmed clay pipe. I also imagined him owning all the land for miles around that would later be worth billions. Actually, he is of Irish-Welsh descent.

11

How Life Insurance Companies Provide Life

Sitting around the long mahogany directors' table in the wood-paneled boardroom of the Detroit Edison Company were Brown, Fisher, and Van Wagoner, the Authority's Executive Committee; Abrams of Allen & Company; and I. The date was November 17, 1953.

Abrams restated the proposition he had made in New York a week earlier. He detailed the scheduling of the Notice of Sale, date of sale, delivery of bonds, meetings, proposed interest rates, and so forth. There was no question about his intent and readiness to go forward with the bridge financing. In fact, he might have been a little too ready for the conservative triumvirate, all bank officers or directors, in whose hands lay the decision to accept or refuse the Allen & Company proposal.

"As you know I have been in contact with the officers of B. J. Van Ingen, and they have assured me that they are not interested at this time," said Abrams.

Brown corroborated the statement by reporting that he had received a letter from Van Ingen's vice-president, James Couffer, informing him that the company could not possibly undertake the bridge matter until after December 31, 1953.

64

"That would be too late," interjected Van Wagoner; "the $417,000 appropriation for maintenance goes out the window if the bonds aren't sold by then."

Brown stated that he had called Couffer and explained this to him and asked if the Authority were free to seek financial advice elsewhere. Brown emphasized that Couffer had replied affirmatively.

"Now we'll have to get a resolution passed by the Authority terminating our agreement."

"I'm ready to go ahead," said Abrams. "Our attorneys are drafting the Notice of Sale and it will be ready for approval by the Authority at its forthcoming meeting on November 24 and could be published in the *Daily Bond Buyer* the next day."

"This is a tentative plan, is it not?" said Fisher, who as president of the National Bank of Detroit had been importuned by several associates to proceed carefully with Allen & Company. There was a pervasive attitude that this company was not big enough to assure the successful sale of the bonds.

"Mr. Abrams," said Brown, "give us another day or two to review the proposition. Can you meet with us the day after tomorrow?"

He assented. The meeting took place in the same room, with the same persons present, and with much of the same discussion as at the previous meeting.

In retrospect, it becomes obvious that the Executive Committee was being unduly hesitant about accepting the proposition proffered. But this did not seem so at the time. The Authority had reason to be cautious. After all, its efforts to finance the structure had been rejected and ignored by the Big Seventeen underwriters that were financing billions of dollars of toll road and bridge construction all over the country; the government's Reconstruction Finance Corporation refused to participate; and Van Ingen had failed twice and would not go to bat the third time.

The members of the Authority, especially Brown and Fisher, were not accustomed to failure. And failure by Allen

& Company would have doomed the project to oblivion for the foreseeable future. No, it would be wiser to forego another attempt to market the bonds than to try to sell them and have the effort fail.

Authority members received no compensation, and they had nothing material to gain by the successful financing. They had a great deal to lose, however. Prentiss M. Brown was a person of immense stature. He had been rated by the Press Corps as one of the ten most effective members of the U.S. Senate. He came within a hair's-breadth of being named Roosevelt's vice-presidential nominee in 1940. He took over the directorship of the Office of Price Administration during World War II when it was bogged down in administrative confusion and public disgust, and he reorganized it into a viable and effective arm of government. He led the Detroit Edison Company through its great postwar financing and construction program.

Charles T. Fisher, Jr., was president of the nation's fourth largest bank. He was a member of the board of directors of the General Motors Corporation, American Airlines, Hiram Walker Distilleries, and a number of educational and religious organizations. His record of public service was one of unparalleled dedication. His awards were many.

Murray D. Van Wagoner had been Michigan's most notable highway commissioner, an elective office, and was rewarded with the governorship. As governor he had presided over the great struggle between the United Automobile Workers and the Ford Motor Company, which was settled without either side engaging in a physical battle, as many had predicted. He also governed Bavaria, West Germany, after World War II. He later served on many commissions and was noted for his unequivocal directness and unusual common sense.

The remaining members of the Authority were also men of stature and probity, men accustomed to getting things done. Now they were struggling to accomplish something that others had attempted and given up for some seventy years—the building of the Mackinac Bridge.

In view of the foregoing facts, it is no wonder that they proceeded with caution—not lack of courage. Thus, only a tentative decision was made on November 19, 1953, to publish the Notice of Sale on November 25. Abrams agreed to cooperate in any way possible. He was aware of the committee's misgivings and apparently decided that patience would be required.

He could have taken umbrage at the suggestion that some other firm manage the financing when he had already taken the lead. The length to which Abrams was willing to go in order to complete the bridge financing is illustrated in an excerpt from the minutes of the November 24, 1953, meeting of the Mackinac Bridge Authority:

> On Monday evening, November 23, Mr. Haggerty of the Metropolitan Life Insurance Company phoned Mr. Fisher and informed him that his company would agree to buy from $7,000,000 to $8,000,000 of Mackinac Bridge bonds, if, in addition to Allen and Company, one of the first line investment bond bankers could be pursuaded to manage the financing. The Smith Barney and Company was mentioned.
>
> In view of all the foregoing developments, Mr. Brown recommended to the members of the Authority that the plan for approving and publishing the Notice of Sale on Wednesday, November 25, 1953, be postponed. He stated that in his opinion it was to the absolute advantage of the Authority that the recommendations of the Metropolitan Life Insurance Company executive be fully explored.
>
> Mr. Abrams stated that notwithstanding the aforementioned developments, his firm was still ready to go ahead and enter a bid on Tuesday, December 1, along with a certified check for $500,000 to guarantee the sale of the bonds. He stated, however, that he would do anything possible to finance the structure and if the Authority felt further negotiation were necessary to insure the financing he would be perfectly willing to cooperate.

Prior to the adjournment of the meeting, a resolution was adopted approving the wording of the Notice of Sale and authorizing the chairman and secretary to decide if and when it should be published.

On November 25, 1953, the day before Thanksgiving,

Brown, Nunneley, our bond counselor, and I met with representatives of Smith Barney & Company. They were polite, prescient, and predictable—predictable in that it was common knowledge that Smith Barney was the principal underwriter of the Indiana Toll Road bonds in the amount of $340,000,000 scheduled for bid opening on December 17, 1953. There was no way that it could undertake the sale of $100,000,000 of Mackinac Bridge bonds until the Indiana bonds were sold.

The selling and distribution of a large bond issue, $100,000,000 or more, requires the full participation of all the parties to such an effort. Brokerage houses which sell to the public, banks which buy for trust portfolios, and insurance companies which invest for their own profits all have to make important decisions evaluating the bond issue, its security, interest yield, their own financial position, and many other factors to reach a decision regarding their participation. The underwriters have an even more formidable task in preparing the information required by the aforementioned parties. Thus, it would have been impossible for Smith Barney to have handled the Indiana Toll Road bonds and the Mackinac Bridge bonds in the same week or ten days, especially with the holiday season at hand.

The only way Smith Barney could join in the sale of Mackinac bonds was for the sale to take place after the first of the year and that meant that the operation and maintenance money would no longer be available.

And that precisely was the tone of the meeting. It is my gut feeling, and it's impossible to corroborate now, that somehow Metropolitan Life got wind of the fact that New York Life was interested in Mackinac Bridge bonds. Whether or not lower level management officers of the two companies engaged in fun and games as to who took the lead position in public project financing only they would know. But it always seemed strange to me that the suggestion to use Smith Barney and the providing of important financial assistance by Metropolitan Life was predicated on terms which in effect would have made the financing impossible. Of course, none of this was even suggested at the meeting. It was agreed that Smith Barney would report back to us within a week or ten days. Brown's personal diary contains the following entry for December 1, 1953: "About 11, Smith Barney chief Hartwig [Cheever Hardwick] called and said while he was satisfied on financing, he was not on the engineering and wanted us to finance a 60 to 90 day examination by another engineer suggesting Greiner of the Chesapeake Bridge. Tough news."

The first documentary evidence in support of a bridge across the Straits of Mackinac appeared in the *Grand Traverse Herald* and was reprinted in the *Lansing Republican* of February 5, 1984. The *Herald* editor, Tom Bates, considered both possibilities, a bridge and a tunnel, practicable. The only question in his mind was that of cost.

William Saulson owned clothing stores in St. Ignace and Newberry. He was a vigorous bridge advocate. On his wrapping paper beneath his portrait appeared a pen-and-ink drawing of the recently opened Brooklyn Bridge. With a bit of promotional license, he had captioned above the picture, "A glimpse of the future" and below it "Proposed Bridge across the Straits of Mackinac." Scribbled on the paper, of which only a photograph now remains, was the date 1884.

THE PEOPLE'S STORE

WILLIAM SAULSON

DRY GOODS

CLOTHING.

A GLIMPSE OF THE FUTURE.

Proposed Bridge across the Straits of Mackinac.

Hats, Caps, Boots, Shoes, Ca... and Oil Cloths.

ST. IGNACE and ... MICH.

The Grand Hotel on Mackinac Island. Commodore Cornelius Vanderbilt, who helped build the hotel, presided over a meeting of its board of directors on July 1, 1888, at which he remarked: "We now have the largest, well equipped hotel of its kind in the world for a short season business. Now what we need is a bridge across the Straits."

As automobiles, once the toys of the rich, were becoming affordable and thus popular, the need to transport them across the Straits arose. Railroad ferries, like the *Sainte Marie*, grudgingly carried them in the early 1920s. This service was expensive at fifteen dollars; inconvenient because gas tanks had to be emptied and headlight lanterns turned off; and time consuming since drivers had to wait hours, if not days, for space on the vessel. Governor Alexander Groesbeck and the state legislature soon recognized the need for better service and ordered the state highway commissioner to establish a regular car ferry operation.

In 1923 the State Highway Department established a car ferry service, and the *Ariel*, which had been ferrying motor vehicles between Detroit and Windsor, was purchased. During its first season of operation, the *Ariel* transported ten thousand automobiles and trucks across the Straits.

As motor car sales increased, so did the demand for Straits crossings. In 1927 the State Highway Department purchased for twenty-five thousand dollars each the *Colonel Card* and the *Colonel Pond*, two World War I ferry boats that had plied Boston Harbor in the service of the War Department. They were renamed the *Sainte Ignace* and the *Mackinaw City*. When World War II broke out, the highway department resold them to the federal government for seventy-five thousand dollars each.

Prentiss M. Brown (*below*).

Chase S. Osborn, the only person from the Upper Peninsula ever elected governor, published the *Sault Ste. Marie Evening News*. He was also a colorful, well-informed man who went to Washington to promote the building of a bridge across the Straits of Mackinac. He saw President Franklin D. Roosevelt and discovered that the president was under the impression that the Straits was "only" twenty or thirty miles wide. Several years later State Highway Commissioner G. Donald Kennedy, then chairman of the Mackinac Straits Bridge Authority, visited the president on the same mission and was very much impressed with his detailed knowledge of Straits geography. Both Osborn and Kennedy won sympathy from Roosevelt, but no support. (Photo courtesy of the Michigan Historical Collections, Bentley Historical Library, University of Michigan.)

The author, as executive secretary of the Mackinac Bridge Authority, is describing some of the features of the proposed bridge to Lieutenant Governor William C. Vandenberg, ca. 1952.

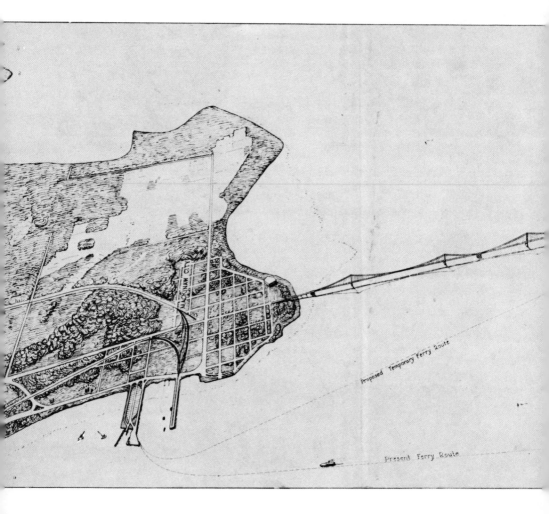

Proposed Temporary Ferry Route

Present Ferry Route

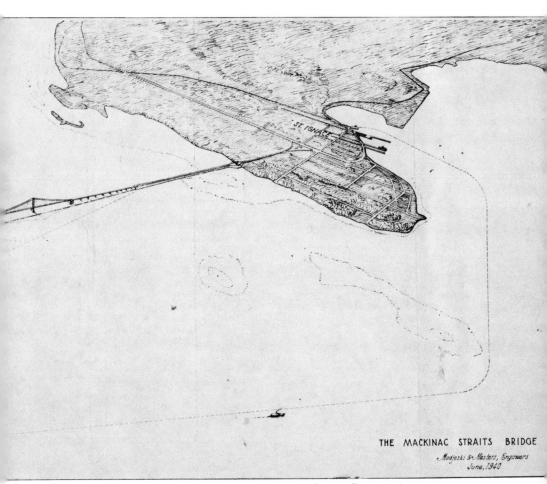

THE MACKINAC STRAITS BRIDGE

Modjeski & Masters, Engineers
June, 1940

Governor Murray D. Van Wagoner and State Highway Commissioner
G. Donald Kennedy had begun the construction of a bridge across the
Straits in the late 1930s. A 4,200-foot-long causeway south into the Straits
from St. Ignace was completed in 1941. This is a drawing of the proposed
bridge. When the United States entered World War II, the bridge was
abandoned.

W. Stewart Woodfill, president, Grand Hotel, on an inspection tour of the bridge two weeks before its opening. He compared the view from the bridge with the view from Amalfi Drive, a statement then widely quoted in the press.

(*Left to right*) W. Stewart Woodfill, comedian Jack Benny, Dr. and Mrs. Birnbaum (friends of Benny), Frank Remly, and the author at the Grand Hotel, Mackinac Island, ca. 1956.

On February 17, 1954, Joseph H. King, president, Union Securities Corporation, handed the author a check for $96,400,033.33, the proceeds of the sale of Mackinac Bridge bonds. It was an auspicious occasion witnessed by most of the people closely connected with the final financing of the project. Seated (*beginning second from left*): Authority members Mead L. Bricker, William J. Cochran, and Charles T. Fisher, Jr.; James S. Abrams, Jr.; D. Hale Brake, state treasurer; Authority chairman Prentiss M. Brown; Joseph H. King; the author holding the $96,400,033.33 check; Charles Darnton, vice-president of Detroit Bank and Trust Company, the trustee; Authority member George Osborn; and Wade Van Valkenburg, speaker, Michigan House of Representatives. Standing: (*seventh from left*) John Mitchell, founder of Mitchell & Pershing; (*tenth from left*) John Nunneley, Authority legal counsel; (*twelfth from left*) Robert Mitchell, bond counselor, Mitchell & Pershing; (*fifth from right*) Norman Downey, vice-president, Union Securities Corporation; and (*fourth from right*) Herbert Goodkind, assistant to David B. Steinman.

James S. Abrams, Jr., vice-president, Allen & Company, recommended the novel financing procedure which made the sale of Mackinac Bridge bonds feasible. Twice before, investment bankers had failed to syndicate the bonds because, according to Abrams, the Authority was trying to raise too much money with a single bond issue. His suggestion to sell first and second lien bonds with different interest rates proved to be the key to success, but not without having to overcome a critical deadline and a lack of Michigan financial support.

Engineers measure the angle of the H-beams driven against the south side of the foundation for Pier 18 to prevent further shift in that direction.

Herman Ellis, Mackinac Bridge photographer, preparing to snap a picture of some operation near the top of the bridge tower.

Governor G. Mennen Williams, accompanied by his wife, Nancy, and members of the Mackinac Bridge Authority, and chauffeured by the author, led the cavalcade of dignitaries and newsmen on the pre-opening inspection tour of the Mackinac Bridge on November 1, 1957.

Posing at the center span during the pre-opening inspection tour of the bridge are (*left to right*): John C. Mackie, state highway commissioner; Dr. David B. Steinman, bridge designer; Governor Williams; Prentiss M. Brown; George A. Osborn and William G. Cochran, Bridge Authority members; and the author.

(*Left to right*) Grover Denny, project manager for Merritt-Chapman & Scott, the foundation contractor; George A. Osborn, publisher of the *Sault Ste. Marie Evening News* and Authority member; David B. Steinman; and Herbert Goodkind, Steinman's assistant.

Prentiss M. Brown, Bridge Authority chairman, receives an album of Mackinac Bridge commemorative stamps from Postmaster General Arthur Summerfield at the bridge dedication luncheon on June 25, 1958. W. Stewart Woodfill and Governor G. Mennen Williams (*far right*) appear to be pleased.

Jack Kinney (*left*), resident engineer, and David B. Steinman (*right*), designer of the Mackinac Bridge, standing on the chain link cable spinning platform.

The chain link fence used to provide a work platform for the cable spinning is prepared for sliding down the five wire ropes which will support it.

Herman Ellis stands on a beam at the tower top waiting for an ore boat to pass under the structure.

Ellis leans backwards over the railing at the tower top to get Miss Michigan in focus for a publicity picture.

The lights installed for the around-the-clock cable spinning operation inspired Prentiss M. Brown and David B. Steinman to make cable lighting a permanent installation on the bridge.

The 1966 Mackinac Bridge walking record (governors' class) is set by Governor George Romney on September 5. Accompanying him (*left to right*) are his state trooper bodyguard and a research assistant, both of whom dog trotted, and the author, who was dog tired.

12

Casting the Die

Critical deadlines were fast approaching. The bonds had to be sold by December 31, 1953. Because of the Christmas holidays, the effective date of this deadline would be December 17. The sale had to be preceded by an advertisement for bids at least a week in advance of the date for accepting them. Thus, the advertisement had to appear in the financial journals no later than December 10, and a day or two prior to that would be required to prepare the ad.

During the week after Thanksgiving, with less than ten days to go, Brown and Fisher met with several Michigan bankers and bond dealers to get some indication of how these bond specialists felt about the Mackinac Bridge issue and the proposed underwriter, Allen & Company. From what I could learn, the reaction of the experts was less than enthusiastic.

Certainly this was true of a meeting I had attended. Several officers of the National Bank of Detroit, the top man at the First of Michigan Corporation, and representatives of one or two other Michigan investment banking houses gathered around a conference table in the old National Bank Building. Each expert expressed his opinion about the probable success of the underwriting. "Failure" would be the more accurate word. Nearly all of them thought that the issue might have a chance if there were more time, if the Authority could wait until after the first of the year. But this was out of the question.

It will be recalled that on November 23, James Haggerty of the Metropolitan Life Insurance Company had suggested to Fisher that his firm would be interested in buying a large block of bonds if one of the first-line investment bond bankers could be persuaded to manage the financing along with Allen & Company.

While the Authority, in keeping with this suggestion, was negotiating unsuccessfully with Smith Barney & Company, the recommendation was also being considered by the ever-practical Abrams. During the week of December 1, the American Bankers Association was meeting at Boca Raton, Florida. Abrams attended it, and somewhere on a golf course, in a bar, or in a smoke-filled room, he came up with three partners, and fairly prestigious ones at that. He phoned Chairman Brown on Wednesday, December 2, to report that Mackinac Bridge financing would be managed by his company along with Union Securities Corporation, Stifel, Nicklaus & Company, and A. C. Allyn Incorporated.

Brown summoned me to his office the next day.

"Larry, time is short. We're going to have to decide whether we should call off the Abrams deal. I want you and John Nunneley to go to New York on Sunday night or early Monday. Arrange a meeting with all the parties concerned: Jim Abrams and his associates, the lawyers, Dave Steinman and Colonel Goodkind, the contractors, the traffic engineers, everybody. Question them in detail about their parts in the proposition. Ascertain every fact that you can. Then call me on Tuesday afternoon at about 2 P.M. and let me know what you and John think. I'll be here with the Executive Committee, and we'll decide on which course to take."

Without his telling me, I realized that he had come to the conclusion that if the bridge were to be financed before the expiration of the $417,000 appropriation, it could only be done by Allen & Company and associates. But he still had—we all did—very real doubts about whether or not these underwriters could successfully do the job. Sometime before December 9 we had to decide either to sell the bonds to Allen & Company or to postpone the Mackinac Bridge project indefinitely—which meant our years of effort would end in failure.

So off we went to New York, where we spent December 7 rounding up the participants for one last thorough and final determination. The meeting was to take place at nine o'clock on Tuesday morning in Allen & Company's conference room on 30 Broad Street.

There was a 100 percent attendance. Nunneley and I followed our instructions and pressed for answers to every possible question that could be raised concerning all facets of the proposed bridge. We made every effort to satisfy ourselves that the parties to the project were being realistic, accurate, capable, and competent. We wanted to ensure that none was interested in the deal for a quick profit, regardless of the outcome.

In retrospect, it was the interrogators who were somewhat biased, at least I was. I wanted the answers to be favorable because, if otherwise, it would have been incumbent upon us to advise the Executive Committee not to go forward with the publication of the Notice of Sale in the December 10 issues of the *Daily Bond Buyer*, a nationally distributed financial publication, the *Wall Street Journal*, and other publications. Then the date of sale could not be seven days later on Thursday, December 17—the last day that it could be approved by the Michigan State Administrative Board before that critical expiration date of December 31.

John Nunneley and I sat at the head of the table. On my left were Steinman and Goodkind. They brought along a thick roll of blueprints which they spread out on the table to support any statements they might make. At this point, Steinman's expenses for the preparation of the bidding plans stood at about $200,000, all paid out of his own pocket. He would lose all of it if the financing failed.

Next to them were William Denny and Charles Richardson, Merritt-Chapman & Scott vice-presidents. Their company was the low bidder on the foundation contract, implementation of which was contingent upon the successful sale of the bonds. Then came Norman Obbard and Carl Sander of the American Bridge Division of the U.S. Steel Corporation, which had the contract to build the superstructure if and when funds were available.

At the opposite end of the table were Abrams and Norman Downey, vice president of Union Securities Corporation, one of the underwriting firms that Abrams brought in to strengthen the bond distribution effort and sale.

It was not deemed necessary to bring in representatives from the other two firms, A. C. Allyn Incorporated and Stifel, Nicklaus & Company, whose main offices were in Chicago. Abrams and Downey were authorized to speak for them and could do so very well.

Robert Mitchell, the brilliant young lawyer from the bond counseling firm of Mitchell & Pershing, which was founded by his father some fifty years earlier, placed his ubiquitous overstuffed briefcase on the table, removed his glasses, and wiped the lenses as he carefully looked around the table making mental notes of all present. He was responsible for the preparation of the eighty-seven-page Trust Indenture—the contract between the Authority and the trustee representing the bond holders. Once he replaced his glasses, he was ready. So was Sam Brown, vice-president of Coverdale & Colpitts, traffic engineering consultants, whose firm specialized in making analyses and predictions of how much traffic a given project would generate. The firm's reputation for conservative predictions, usually less traffic than was actually realized, made Wall Street investors place great faith in their reports. However, in the case of the Mackinac Bridge—to be built in northern Michigan, connecting Mackinaw City, population nine hundred, with St. Ignace, population three thousand, and three hundred miles from any large metropolitan area—that faith was being severely tested.

We started with Dr. Steinman. For a man of small stature, fitting the stereotype of the old-time college professor, he was always a surprise when he spoke. His words sounded as though they were being cast in bronze. There was absolutely no question about the physical safety of the structure, he said. The foundations were designed to support the superstructure and any live load it would carry by a safety factor of four. The steel superstructure, in turn, would withstand wind pressure of 50 pounds per square foot, or wind velocities up to 125 miles per hour. The highest velocity ever recorded at the Straits was 78 miles per hour. Insofar as torsion was concerned—the weakness that brought down the Tacoma Narrows Bridge in 1940 in a wind of only 42 miles per hour—he told us not to worry. The Mackinac Bridge would not be subject to twisting. Extrapolation of wind tunnel tests of sectional models of the bridge as designed proved that even with winds of infinite velocity there would be no torsional vibration, or absorption of energy from the wind, a condition that spelled doom for many bridges in the past.

This was all very complicated, but no one doubted that the good doctor knew what he was talking about. It was true that in this area of bridge deck vibration, Steinman was ahead of his contemporaries, some of whom ridiculed his demonstrations, which made it easy for laymen to visualize the difference between a bridge design with built-in twisting problems and one without them.

"What about schedule, Doctor?" I asked. The Authority financing plans covered the cost of interest for four years. "You say that the bridge can be completed in forty-two months. You know the weather at the Straits can be pretty rough, and the waters too. We'll have to close down during the winter. Do you really think it can be done? Because if the bridge isn't opened for traffic on November 1, 1957, as you predict, then we'll be in serious trouble in meeting our interest payments without any revenues coming in."

Again Steinman voiced complete conviction in the reality of his schedule, but deferred to the contractors who would have to carry it out. Denny spoke first. He stated that his firm planned to use the largest fleet of construction vessels ever assembled for a project of this kind and that he was confident that his firm could build the thirty-three marine foundations as planned. He was questioned about the anchor blocks in which the ends of the cables would be secured. Building them involved the pouring of a record quantity of concrete that had to be completed in one operation. It was estimated that it would take thirty-one days to make such a pour. He was asked if he realized that the weather at the Straits is such that it storms about every ten days. These were storms that would require their vessels to seek safe harbor and therefore necessitate a break in the pouring operation.

Denny stated that he and his colleagues were aware of the problem and had solved it by their intention to use the Pre-Pakt concrete intrusion method for the anchor blocks. In response to our raised eyebrows, he explained in simple terms that the aggregates, or small stones which are generally mixed with the cement and water to make concrete, would instead be placed in the foundation cofferdam or form. Then, through previously erected pipes inside the cofferdam, the grout (a mixture of cement, water, and fly ash) would be pumped into the aggregates, completely surrounding them to form concrete. This procedure would allow the contractor to break off the concreting process whenever necessary without damaging the strength or integrity of the foundation. Steinman nodded his assent.

Insofar as the superstructure was concerned, it was, relatively speaking, the easier part of the job. Obbard stated that once the Authority had the funds for the project, American Bridge would start rolling and fabricating the steel necessary for the stiffening trusses and towers at Ambridge, near Pittsburgh. The order was already on the books, he said, and scheduled to begin in March to coincide with the expected delivery date of the bonds and the receipt of a check for the sale thereof. But, Sander cautioned, if the money were not on hand, then the fixed amount of the contract, contingent upon the successful sale of the bonds, would have to be revised upward due to inflationary pressure.

There were not too many questions we could address to this contractor. We knew the reputation of U.S. Steel, and the superstructure design called for construction techniques with which the American Bridge Division was well experienced.

We moved to Mitchell, who reviewed the highlights of the Trust Indenture explaining in layman's language the highly technical and legalistic provisions that protect the bond buyers' investment, thus making the bonds attractive, while loading full responsibility for that investment security on the Authority. They boiled down to the following requirements: that interest and principal payments and contributions to reserve funds will be met on schedule; that tolls will be established at rates sufficient to provide revenues to meet the aforementioned obligations as well as the cost of operation, maintenance, and repair; that the bridge will be run efficiently and economically; that it will be inspected annually by reputable consulting engineers; that records of all traffic, revenues, and expenditures will be reported monthly; that the accounts will be examined quarterly by outside auditors during construction and semiannually thereafter; that property damage and liability insurance will be obtained; and that budgets will be prepared annually and approved by the consulting engineers, the trustee, and the principal underwriter. The provisions covered every facet of bridge operation and finance. Mitchell said that the Trust Indenture was ready. He had consulted with lawyers representing insurance companies that might purchase large blocks of the bonds, and they were satisfied that their clients would have full protection. He said he had drafted all the resolutions, about ten in number, that would have to be adopted by the Authority and the State Administrative Board in connection with the sale and approval of the bond issue. He cautioned once again that if the sale were not completed by December 31, he would have to rewrite a substantial portion of the

Trust Indenture. Though he was the youngest man at the table, he was as sound and serious and convincing as any of us attending the meeting.

It was Brown's turn, and if ever there were a shoal on which to founder, it was the prediction of future bridge traffic. In this case, there were more than the usual hazards: the rural location of the bridge and the fact that there was roughly a four-year lapse between the time the predictions were made and the time the bridge would open. Anything could happen.

"Well, Sam, in your updated report you say that the convenience of the bridge vis-à-vis the present ferry service will induce an 85 percent increase in Straits crossings. Do you still feel confident of this prediction and do you think hard-nosed bond dealers around the country will buy it?" I asked.

"To answer the last part first," said Brown, "hard-nosed bond dealers, investment bankers, and government fund managers have been buying our predictions since 1883. We haven't been right all the time, but we have a pretty good track record. As far as Mackinac is concerned, we believe our 85 percent figure is pretty conservative. After all, we did come down from 125 percent induced traffic in our original report made two years ago."

That raised a good question. Why did Coverdale & Colpitts reduce that estimate, we wanted to know. When their original report said that Straits traffic would more than double in the first year of operation, even members of the Authority were skeptical. Prentiss Brown later related a story of how, a year before this meeting, the president of Coverdale & Colpitts, George Burpee, was by sheer accident seated at the same table as he in the dining car of a train from Washington, D.C., to New York. Brown discussed the firm's Mackinac Bridge estimates of traffic growth and said he thought they were too high. Burpee responded that he would look into the matter. Subsequently, the figure for induced traffic was reduced 40 percentage points, from 125 percent to 85 percent.

Brown's explanation was not entirely satisfying. He

pointed out that when the first report was prepared, the ferry fare was $1.75 for a passenger car. The assumption was made that the bridge tolls would be roughly the same. At that rate, Coverdale & Colpitts predicted that the crossings would more than double in the first year of operation. However, in the interim between the first and the most recent report, the ferry rate had been increased to an average of $3.40 per car and passengers. Since the bridge toll would now have to be raised accordingly, to $3.25 per car, fewer motorists would be induced to make the trip. Hence the downward revision. We accepted Brown's explanation, but I have always had the nagging thought that Coverdale & Colpitts looked at what was necessary in terms of annual revenues to make the project acceptable to underwriters, and then decided on an induced traffic percentage increase to meet those revenues. It is altogether possible that I am doing an injustice to the firm, and if so, I do humbly withdraw the above.*

Now it came down to the all-important question. Abrams and Downey were attentive to the preceding discussions, occasionally throwing in a question of their own.

"Okay, Jim and Norm, you've heard it all. Do you still think you can peddle these bonds?"

"If we didn't think so," they replied, "we wouldn't be here." But the actual dialogue was not that simple. We reviewed their entire plan for syndicating the bonds with special emphasis on how much had been committed by institutional buyers, largely insurance companies. There was a rule of thumb that if institutional purchases had not accounted for at least 50 percent of the issue, then it was not likely to be a successful sale. Of course, when it came to the Mackinac Bridge issue, previous rules and guidelines were often not applicable.

---

*Traffic during 1958, the first full year of operation, was up only 50 percent. I saw Sam Brown at a toll facility association meeting in 1962, and I asked him how Coverdale & Colpitts could have been so far off in its predictions. He gave me a rather cold look and replied, "Hell, you got your bridge, didn't you?" To which I say, amen.

"This is a unique proposition," said Abrams. "First, you've got a project being built in a rural area that should be in a metropolitan area. Second, it has a record-breaking price, a $100,000,000 issue for a bridge. The Golden Gate was only $36,000,000. Third, it has seasonal traffic. Fourth, the Straits of Mackinac allegedly encompasses the roughest water on the Great Lakes, and you are planning thirty-three marine foundations in that water. Fifth, the Michigan legislature has provided only token support for the project. Now you ask, 'Can we sell the bonds?'"

Abrams paused. His eyes narrowed, his jaw jutted out. "And our answer is, you're damned well right we can."

Downey, gray, studious, very deliberate and slow speaking, added that they would not undertake the project if they were not sure they could succeed. They were well aware of all the drawbacks but had assessed the situation carefully and with the resources of the four underwriters now managing the bond sale, they were confident they would succeed. It would not be a pushover, but it would be done. We pressed for a figure on institutional purchases, but they refused to speculate except to assure us that they would be adequate. We discussed the time schedule, and it was at this point that they were adamant. A decision must be reached within twenty-four hours so that they could prepare, as required by law, the advertisement of the Notice of Sale.

The questioning continued throughout lunch, which was brought in. Finally Nunneley and I reached a decision. We called Brown at his Detroit Edison office.

"Mr. Brown," I reported, "John and I have been meeting until just a few minutes ago with all the parties you recommended. We have questioned them in detail pursuant to your instructions, and we have both reached the conclusion that the Authority should go forward with the Notice of Sale on December 10."

There was a long pause.

"Larry, Mr. Fisher and Mr. Van Wagoner" (not "Chick" and "Pat," as he usually called them) "are on phone extensions, and I am sure they have heard your report and your recommendation."

There was another pause. It seemed interminable.

"We have considered what you said, and we have decided that you should place the Notice of Sale."

The die was cast.

The Last-Minute Bridge Block

The Honorable D. Hale Brake, Republican state treasurer, was deeply engrossed in thought—his forte. Brake was not much of a talker, but he certainly could think, and clearly, too. Now, he was carefully weighing the suggestions of the men seated around his desk regarding the best procedure for killing the sale of Mackinac Bridge bonds scheduled to take place the next day.

Legs crossed, hands clasped under his chin, the taciturn Brake leaned back in his overstuffed leather chair, alternately closing and opening his eyes to gaze out the window. Dominating his view was the snowcapped head of Michigan's Civil War governor Austin Blair, whose larger-than-life statue towered above the concrete walkway to the front entrance of the state capitol.

Brake would vow to his dying day that he was not opposed to the Mackinac Bridge, providing it would not be a "financial burden to the people of Michigan." In fact, he surprised a good many of his critics when he spoke at the assembly of the nation's underwriters in New York in March 1953 and stated that the Mackinac Bridge was not a "political football," but that it had been endorsed at both the Democratic and Republican conventions. This endorsement pleased Democratic governor G. Mennen Williams, but not some skeptics like me, who lunched daily with several state treasury officials. They spoke freely about Brake's position that the bridge ought to be financed with state-backed general obligation bonds to achieve lower interest rates. An admirable goal, but it would require a vote of the people at the next general election. Anybody who believed that Michigan voters, who reside largely in the southern part of the state, would take on a debt of $100,000,000 for a bridge three hundred miles away also believed that Paul Bunyan was alive and logging in Newberry. Brake was an astute politician. He knew that a general obligation bond was out of the question.

He also knew that if the bridge were built now, during the Democratic administration of Governor Williams, the Democrats would take eternal credit for it.

It is only fair to note that there were sincere misgivings about the soundness of the bridge project. Many persons thought it would be a burden on the taxpayers. Was Brake's opposition to the project motivated by his GOP loyalties or his conviction that the bridge would be a white elephant?

Perhaps this is what he was pondering while gazing out his window. Should he help plot some devious scheme to spoil the effort? Should he let it be and then be in a position to say "I told you so" when the bridge costs overran or the lack of revenues required Authority members to come hat in hand to the legislature for money to bail out the project?

But what if the bridge should be a success? Brake was no doubt weighing all aspects as he watched the snow fall on the Civil War governor. His lieutenants assured him less than a year before that nobody would ever buy Mackinac Bridge bonds, and for many months it had appeared that they would be right. Even after the legislature had appropriated funds for operation, maintenance, and repair to prove that the state supported the project, the second proposed bond sale had failed. So maybe his advisors were correct. He would never invest any of the state's several funds in bridge bonds. Would any other sound investor do so?

It appeared that some would, sound investment or not. On the next day, December 17, 1953, the Authority was scheduled to receive bids on the bonds being offered. He knew that an underwriter's representative had arrived in Lansing with a check in hand to make a sizable no-return deposit to accompany his bid. What was he to do?

"It'll never go," declared one advisor, punctuating his position by stamping out his cigarette in the souvenir ashtray that graced the glass top of the treasurer's desk along with a few neat stacks of papers and reports and an unfolded copy of the *Wall Street Journal*.

Brake's gaze was still fixed on the old governor. "That's what you said last April when the $417,000 appropriation for maintenance was in the legislature. Now here we are right down to the deadline and it looks to me like they've got a sale."

"That's true," argued another advisor. "They may have a bid and get a deposit. But they'll never peddle those bonds in Michigan. Not if word gets around that the state's own treasurer thinks they're a poor risk. And if Michigan dealers don't buy them, nobody will."

"You underestimate Brown and Fisher," Brake said. "Originally it was only Allen & Company bidding on the issue. But Brown and Fisher insisted that they align themselves with additional investment bankers and now it's Allen, Union Securities, Stifel Nicklaus—which has Mott backing—and A. C. Allyn. I would say that's a formidable team."

"I think you're right, Brake."

It was Senator Haskell Nichols, the balding, bespectacled, cigar-chewing chairman of the Senate Highways Committee. Now he was a talker: not always right, not always wrong, but always willing to take a position, when he sensed which way the wind was blowing. Nichols was benignly dubbed by his friends the "Senator Claghorn of the North." He was a likeable fellow, ready to accommodate the underdog, his fellow senators, lobbyists, whomever. Now he was trying to help the state treasurer and the state highway commissioner. Senator Nichols could not have cared less whether the bridge were built. His Jackson constituency was more than two hundred miles from the Straits. He never voted against it because, like so many of his colleagues, he thought it could never be financed or built anyway.

So, chewing on his ever-present cigar, which his doctor told him he must never light, Nichols announced that he had a plan.

"I can petition the Supreme Court to prohibit the State Administrative Board from approving the sale of the bonds on Thursday on the grounds that the legislation is flawed."

There was a flicker of interest in Brake's cold, blue eyes. He turned toward Nichols.

"I'm sure the justices will accommodate me as a courtesy to a senator and a lawyer. I'll get my petition in the first thing tomorrow morning. They'll act on it before the Ad Board meeting on Thursday. That means the receiving of the bids will be nullified and approval of the sale indefinitely postponed."

The treasurer's eyes crinkled a bit, and the trace of a smile betrayed his normally stern expression.

"What good will that do?" demanded one of the advisors.

"By the time the matter can be brought before the full court, and new bids advertised for and received, it will be after December 31, 1953, and the $417,000 maintenance appropriation will expire." Nichols puffed triumphantly but vainly on his unlit cigar. "Without that appropriation, the bond sale will be dead and the bridge financing stalled indefinitely."

Brake rose from his chair, pulled down the coat of his double-breasted, navy-blue serge suit, adjusted his unframed glasses, and was about to speak when Highway Commissioner Charles M. Ziegler, a little slow on the uptake, said, "Sounds good to me, Haskell. What do you think, Hale?"

"The worst," said Brake, addressing himself to the senator, "is that you'll be accused of sabotaging the project."

"That's not so," replied the senator. "All I'll be doing is testing the legality of the bond issue. It should be tested. There are many questions, such as whether gas and weight tax money can be used to maintain the bridge."

The senator had a point, not a very good one, but just enough to rationalize his action in the event he was questioned by the press.

So partly out of concern for the constitutionality of the bridge legislation and partly out of concern for good roads, the senator was eager to go forward with his petition. His collaborators agreed that it was a good idea and solely his idea. They wanted no part of it. When they ran for election, their constituency would be statewide, and in no way would they risk the criticism of having destroyed the bridge financing.

The fourteen-foot-high ceiling with its rococo trimmings, the thick mahogany casements surrounding the windows, and the carpet decorated with the repetitive design of the state's outline all began to look good to the state treasurer. He beamed inwardly as he focused on the wall where the photographs of his predecessors hung and imagined his own countenance there one day. He imagined even more. He imagined himself upstairs in the executive office, running the state on a conservative pay-as-you-go basis with the whole country applauding the farm boy who had pulled himself up from his humble beginnings to be the efficient chief executive of the seventh largest state in the Union.

And indeed he did run for governor several years later. He came in fourth or fifth in the Republican primary. No one seems to remember.

So with the silent acquiescence of his co-conspirators, Senator Nichols did present his petition to the Supreme Court and called a press conference to explain his action. His stated intention—to test the validity of the legislation—made the early headlines and noonday broadcasts.

The Courtly Court

Brown's grip on the steering wheel tightened; he drove a shade faster than usual. He was a fighter, determined, tenacious, and he was not going to lose this project. He spoke no more. Marian could see in his profile the expression she had seen many times before. Here was a man who took on President Roosevelt at the height of his popularity when he attempted to pack the U.S. Supreme Court, to increase its membership, in order to gain favorable opinions for his executive orders and legislation.

Brown opposed the move as a matter of principle, but his position was a lonely one in the U.S. Senate, which had become accustomed to supporting the president in virtually all his efforts to end the Great Depression as well as some of the abuses that brought it on. Roosevelt accused "the nine old men," the Supreme Court justices, of blocking his progress.

To solve the problem, the president asked Congress to increase the court membership from nine to thirteen. He would then appoint four new justices sympathetic to his view and thereby obviate any majority of negative votes on his proposals. This court-packing scheme was repugnant to several members of the Senate, and, in due course, they were successful in persuading a majority of the members that they were right. Brown was one of the leaders of the loyal opposition. It fell upon him to inform the president of the United States that the Senate would not pass his legislation to pack the court. It was no small task. If ever there were a beneficent dictator, Roosevelt was he, especially in those early days when the entire country was, so to speak, eating out of his hand. But Brown was equal to the task. Although he admired and respected the president, referred to him as his Chief, and was in full accord with his program, it was his conviction that the great tradition of the Supreme Court should not be sacrificed on the altar of expedience. He confronted the president with his position and despite the blandishments, arguments, and, perhaps, implied threats of the nation's most powerful and persuasive leader in decades, Brown did not waver. The court was not packed.

Now it was another court matter and by the time he reached Lansing, Brown had formulated his battle plan. Accompanied by John Nunneley, the Authority's legal counsel, who was already in Lansing for the next day's events, he went directly to the office of the clerk of the State Supreme Court, who was a friend, and asked if any of the members were still in their offices.

"Yes," replied the clerk, "Chief Justice Dethmers and several associates are still here. What can I do for you, Senator?"

"I would like a brief meeting with them at their convenience this afternoon. It is a matter of the utmost importance."

The meeting took place.

The men sat around the conference table of the high-ceilinged office adjacent to the Supreme Court chambers in the capitol building. The members of the court sat on one side, and Brown and Nunneley sat on the other.

"Gentlemen," said Brown after the opening amenities had been observed, "I have not had a chance to read and study Senator Nichols's petition in depth, but I am convinced, and John Nunneley concurs, that if you grant his petition now, bridge financing will be destroyed for the present and foreseeable future."

Brown then explained that unless the bonds were sold by December 31, 1953, the legislation granting $417,000 annually for operation and maintenance would expire. Without that appropriation, the state's relatively small gesture of interest in the project, the bonds would be difficult, if not impossible, to sell.

Brown pointed out that he did not object to testing the validity of the bond sale, the legislation, or any other facet of the bridge proposition, but he respectfully requested that the justices permit the sale of the bonds to take place; allow the Authority and the Administrative Board to conduct business relative thereto; and thereby not destroy many, many years of hard work by hundreds of persons without a full hearing on the matter.

He made it clear that the bonds would not be delivered nor the proceeds of their sale received until February 17, 1954. In the meantime, said Brown, briefs could be prepared and filed, arguments heard, and a decision handed down by the full court. If indeed it was found that Nichols's arguments were justified, then the Supreme Court could prohibit the Authority from delivering the bonds and the effect would be the same as if the petition were granted today, before the sale of the bonds.

The justices listened attentively. They asked questions. They conferred quietly among themselves. Brown's arguments were convincing. He was willing to give Nichols his day in court. Certainly, the least they could do was give Brown his day in court, too. They would also give the people their day in court by conducting a full hearing on the matter.

Senator Nichols's petition was temporarily denied.

15

The Twenty-Five Minute Bridge

December 17, 1953, dawned a dull, cold day, but by noon the sun was shining on one of the most significant events in Michigan history.

According to a public notice that had appeared in the December 10 issue of the *Daily Bond Buyer*, $99,800,000 of Mackinac Bridge bonds would be offered for sale in the executive office of the state capitol at Lansing. Sealed bids would have to be in the hands of the secretary of the Authority before 10:00 A.M. eastern standard time. Any bid submitted would have to be accompanied by a certified check for $100,000 as a matter of good faith on the part of the bidder. The Authority could legally keep the money if the bidder failed to complete the bond purchase.

Interested parties began gathering outside the governor's office at 9:00 A.M. I was nervous. Brown and Van Wagoner were in town, but had not yet arrived. Fisher was scheduled to drive up from Detroit. Cochran, who had the farthest to come, about 450 miles from Iron Mountain, wired that he would be there if he had to come by dogsled. There was no word from George Osborn, Authority member from northern Sault Ste. Marie. Mead Bricker, another Authority member, could not make it, and Highway Commissioner Ziegler was conveniently out of town. Two members were present, and three more were expected. Four were required for a quorum. Imagine the irony of the situation if, after all the Authority had been through, after seventy years of trying, there were not enough members present to legally approve the sale of the bonds that would pay for bridge construction. It was enough to cause palpitations.

Then, Cochran came in. A long distance call from Osborn with the news that his flight had been cancelled at the last minute was disheartening. But Fisher showed up at 9:30. Then Brown and Van Wagoner entered the governor's outer office. Along with them was Jim Abrams, vice-president of Allen & Company, the man with the bid. He in turn was accompanied by his associates: Joseph D. Murphy of Stifel, Nicklaus & Company, and Norman Downey, vice-president of Union Securities Corporation. Now that a quorum was present, along with the principal underwriters who handed me their envelope containing the bid, I breathed more freely. Yet there was an air of tenseness—history was in the making—about the room, as state officers, legislators, news reporters, and photographers drifted in and out. It seemed as though the impossible were about to take place: the Mackinac Bridge was really on the verge of being financed.

Twice I checked with the telephone operator to ascertain that the wall clock was correct. It seemed an eternity until the minute hand finally made it up to the twelve. I asked if there were any more bids to be submitted on Mackinac Bridge bonds. My voice was nervously high-pitched and hardly rose above the din of the crowd.

Prentiss Brown was cool. He stood at the head of a table placed in the office for the Authority's use and calmly invited the members to sit down. Upon my assurance that a quorum was present, he asked that this official meeting of the Mackinac Bridge Authority please come to order.

Cochran moved and Van Wagoner supported a motion to dispense with the reading of the minutes of the previous meeting. It passed unanimously. There were no reports of officers or committees. Brown carefully followed the meeting procedure prescribed by the bylaws. There were no comments. Everybody wanted to get to the business at hand. Chairman Brown stated that on the agenda "under unfinished business" there was the matter of the sale of Mackinac Bridge bonds. One would think he was talking about the disposition of a surplus desk.

I stated that I had received one sealed bid prior to 10:00 A.M. on December 17, 1953. The chairman then asked me to open the bid and read it. It stated that the Allen & Company management group had bid an interest rate of 4 percent on the Authority's offering of $79,800,000 of Series A bonds and 5.25 percent on $20,000,000 of Series B bonds. The total proceeds of the bid to the Authority would be $95,858,000, which was $50,000 above the 4 percent maximum discount allowed in the Authority's Notice of Sale. I later learned that at dinner the night before, Brown had prevailed upon Abrams not to bid the "bare bones," as Brown put it, even though it was virtually guaranteed that there would be no competitive bid. Abrams generously agreed to the suggestion and bid accordingly.

The bid was accompanied by a certified check for $100,000, dated December 16, 1953, and drawn on the Chase National Bank of New York. John Nunneley, the Authority's Michigan bond counsel, and Robert Mitchell, the New York bond counsel, examined the bid papers and declared that the bid was proper.

Brown then stated that before the bid could be accepted and approved, the Authority would have to approve a resolution authorizing the issuance of the bonds and the execution and delivery of the Trust Indenture. The latter is the contract between the Authority and the representative of the bond holders, usually a bank, and in this case, the Detroit Bank and Trust Company. The Trust Indenture sets forth all the requirements of the Authority pertaining to the construction, operation, and maintenance of the bridge; the handling and disposition of all revenues; and the setting of tolls—in all, eighty-seven pages of fine print designed to make sure that the bond holders and the investors would not only get the loans repaid but would also receive the stipulated rate of tax-exempt interest every six months for forty years or until the debt was retired, whichever came first. It was then moved by Van Wagoner and seconded by Fisher that the issuance of the bonds and the execution and delivery of the Trust Indenture be approved. The motion carried unanimously.

All the while, observers listened carefully to the proceedings. Reporters took notes and photographers hovered about, clicking and flashing. They were reporting the news and recording history.

But it was not over!

The sale of the bonds still had to be approved by the State Administrative Board. The members of that board were gathered around a table in Governor Williams's office where they usually met every other Tuesday morning. They had conducted their routine business two days earlier, on December 15, and had recessed until this morning for the sole purpose of acting on the sale of the Mackinac Bridge bonds.

The governor called the meeting to order. Prentiss Brown had recessed the Mackinac Bridge Authority meeting and was now present at the Administrative Board meeting, where he was called upon by the governor. Brown stated that the sale of $99,800,000 of Mackinac Bridge bonds had been consummated and respectfully requested the State Administrative Board to approve that sale as was required under section five of Public Act 214 of 1952. This approval was needed before the bonds could be delivered and funds received.

D. Hale Brake, a member of the Administrative Board, requested a brief recess so that the Republican members of the board could caucus. Governor Williams granted the recess, stating that it was the first time in history that such a caucus took place. We waited, wondering what was happening. The majority of the members of the board were Republicans, but they would not thwart the bridge effort now—or so we thought. Fortunately, the caucus was brief. The members returned to their seats and perfunctorily moved, seconded, and unanimously approved the sale of the bonds.

The Bridge Authority meeting then resumed. The Authority unanimously adopoted resolutions awarding and selling the bonds; allowing the secretary to sign each bond with his first two initials and surname rather than his full name (an energy and time saving gesture since 99,800 individual bonds would have to be signed); permitting officers to sign requisitions; ratifying the Executive Committee's action in contracting with the American Bridge Division of the U.S. Steel Corporation to build the entire superstructure at a firm price of $44,532,900 (the largest contract ever undertaken by that company to date); and finally, approving the Executive Committee's action in entering into a contract with Merritt-Chapman & Scott to build the bridge foundations at a fixed cost of $25,735,600.

There was no other business to discuss. Enough had already been done. The meeting adjourned at 10:25 A.M., less than half hour an after it commenced. Three and a half years of toil and tears were finally wrapped up in a triumphal twenty-five minutes.

Or were they?

16

Sabotage!

The year promised to end on a gala note. The bridge bonds had been sold. The contingency construction contracts had been awarded. Now, all we had to do was sit back while the bonds were being printed and the contractors were involved with the logistics of transporting men, materials, and machinery to the Straits of Mackinac.

The scheduling was excellent. As soon as the holidays were over, the principal underwriter would be telephoning and writing to stock and bond brokers all over the country to form a syndicate that would ultimately sell the bonds to institutions and the public. The brokers would also approach insurance companies and banks to obtain commitments for purchases of large blocks of bonds. On February 17, 1954, a full-page advertisement would appear in the *Wall Street Journal* and the *Detroit Free Press* offering the bonds for sale to the public. The names of all the firms handling the bonds (there were eventually eighty-seven of them) would be printed in the lower portion of the ad. (As a result, such display advertisements came to be known as the "gravestone ads.")

In the meantime, 99,800 individual bonds, each with eighty coupons attached, had to be printed. At that time, only two companies in the United States were equipped to carry out such an assignment. Security had to be as tight as though it were the government mint, because these were bearer bonds and whoever possessed them could keep them or cash their coupons without the necessity of explaining how they were obtained. Also, on February 17, 1954, the Authority would ceremoniously deliver the bonds to the underwriters and receive in return a check for the amount of their bid plus the interest that had accumulated since January 1, 1954. The contractors would be ready to begin as soon as the Straits was ice free. Groundbreaking ceremonies were scheduled for St. Ignace and Mackinaw City on May 7th and 8th.

Sometime along the way the bonds would have to be individually signed by a representative of Detroit Bank and Trust, the trustee, and by me as secretary of the Authority. We were scheduled to go to New York to complete this chore in late January. It was to be done at the Signature Signing Company, a rather unpretentious operation on the sixth floor of one of the older buildings buried deep in New York's financial district. To our relief, we found out that we would not have to write our names 99,800 times because the company had developed a signature device equipped with ten pens. It was delicately balanced so that by guiding the pen in hand and signing one bond, nine others were simultaneously signed. It took some practice to get accustomed to handling the master pen, but in due course it was accomplished, and we had to sign our names only 9,980 times. Nevertheless, it took the better part of three days and caused some mild discomfort otherwise known as writer's cramp.

On December 24, 1953, several friends and I journeyed to my cabin in the Caberfae ski area near Cadillac, intending to enjoy a very merry Christmas and the happiest of new years. The skiing was great and the camaraderie warm. Many acquaintances familiar with the three-year-long bridge struggle dropped by to express their congratulations and good wishes.

There was one visitor, however, from the Saginaw-Bay

City area, who remarked about some problems our underwriters had encountered in Michigan. We paid little heed to his comments because we thought there would be no action until after New Year's and because we knew there would always be someone ready to throw cold water on the proposition.

The first call we received upon returning to Lansing after the week-long holiday was from Jim Abrams.

"What the hell's going on there?" There was no chuckle in his voice. "Somebody is sabotaging our deal in Michigan."

It was true. Only one brokerage firm in the entire state of Michigan was willing to join the bond-distributing syndicate.*

Abrams asked me to come to New York, where he put it to me straight: "Somebody in Michigan is squashing this deal. Buyers sense that there is something wrong because of the lack of home-state broker support. To make matters worse, we're faced with competition. Indiana Turnpike bonds, which were also sold on the 17th, are coming out and even though they pay less interest, buyers like them because turnpikes are more attractive investments than bridges, especially since Mackinac is up in the boondocks. And if that weren't enough, experts are of the opinion that we are on the verge of a new era of higher interest rates. Nobody wants to make long term commitments until they see which way these rates will go."

We had other problems. The prospectus, which must be scrupulously prepared so that no aspect of the proposition could be misrepresented, failed to state who would determine bridge employees' wage and salary scales—the Authority or the Michigan Civil Service. In preparing the prospectus it was deemed advisable to omit this information because the Michigan Supreme Court was at the time weigh-

---

*Only John Kenower, of Kenower, MacArthur & Company, had defied the apparent disenchantment with Mackinac Bridge bonds. Later, Kenower told me it was the best decision he ever made, and that the company profited handsomely by its participation.

ing the matter in connection with litigation involving the Michigan Turnpike Authority, an agency structured very much like the Mackinac Bridge Authority. Now the omission began to haunt us because rumors were afloat that someone might challenge the bond issue in court. Underwriters are constantly on tenterhooks because of the possibility of an overlooked detail, and this omission justified their fears. Any opponent with a few dollars could start a legal action, and a sympathetic judge could delay the entire proposition. The mere threat of such litigation was probably discouraging purchase commitments by potential members of the bond-selling syndicate.

Fortunately, nobody decided to litigate on the salary matter or any other matter, serious or frivolous.

As for the other difficulties, they were real and present, but we eventually overcame them. First, Senator Nichols's objection to the bond sale had to be dealt with. This bad news was revealed in Brown's diary on January 21, 1954: "Nichols now introduces bill to have referendum on Mackinac Bridge. Silly as ever." The good news was that after the filing of briefs and a full hearing on the Nichols petition, the Supreme Court voted unanimously to deny it. Interest rates did indeed begin to rise shortly after the bonds were sold, and they have never dropped to the level of February 1954. Had not the bonds been sold when they were, it is certain that they never would have been, unless the legislature were willing to guarantee them with the state's faith and credit or with the backing of the Motor Vehicle Highway Fund, which is made up of the receipts of gasoline and license plate taxes.

The delivery of the bonds went smoothly on February 17, 1954. Until then, there were a great many persons figuratively holding their breaths. The ceremony occurred in a walnut-paneled conference room of the Union Securities offices. Surrounded by Authority members, state officials, consulting engineers, contractors, underwriters, attorneys, bankers, and photographers, Prentiss Brown was handed a check for $96,400,033.33. After posing for pictures, Brown

111

handed the check to me to deposit with the trustee. D. Hale Brake endorsed it as state treasurer and so did I, as secretary. However, before giving it to the trustee, I held the check in my pocket for fifteen minutes. During that time it earned $125 in interest.*

---

*Had the bridge been financed in 1983, it would have required a bond issue of $350,000,000 at an interest rate of 10 percent. The check would have earned, during that fifteen-minute period, more than $900. To pay off this bond issue, the bridge fare would have to be about $30 per vehicle.

17

The Thirty-Foot Move

The first check written by the Authority was to the order of David B. Steinman in the amount of $280,000. The members of the Authority were unanimous in their gratitude and if there were any honor or distinction in his receiving the first check, we all felt that he deserved it. He responded with a generous gesture by informing the Authority that his fee would be limited to $3,500,000 rather than the customary percentage of the construction cost, which would have meant a greater return for him, especially if there were overruns, as everyone expected there would be.

The second order of business was implementing the two major construction contracts, which were contingent upon the successful sale of the bonds. The Authority agreed to pay the American Bridge Division $44,532,900 to fabricate and erect the steel superstructure. The amount was $3,000,000 less than the bid of the Bethlehem Steel Company, the only other contractor offering to build the superstructure. Several firms were invited to bid on the foundations. Merritt-Chapman & Scott of New York was the low bidder and after negotiation agreed on a fixed cost of $25,735,600 with no escalation whatsoever. This was an important consideration in the marketing of the bonds. There are a great many unknowns and uncertainties in performing work underwater and with waterborne equipment. No matter how many soundings or borings are made, working underwater is not the same as being able to survey the terrain underfoot; and when it comes to working out on the water versus solid ground, the risks multiply progressively. Unforeseen extra costs can become a major source of overruns. So long as these increased costs can occur, the financing problem becomes difficult, if not impossible. Funds set aside for contingencies, if too high, add to the problem of bond selling. If too low, then money runs out and the project may have to be shut down before completion—and even be abandoned.

Before February 1954 ended, the contractors had already moved into the Straits area. Merritt-Chapman & Scott set up recruiting offices in St. Ignace, negotiated for storage and dock space, and made arrangements with local suppliers for a variety of items that could not be economically obtained by its New York purchasing department. A dozen or more subcontractors were engaged to perform various operations: boring into the underlying rock formations; surveying to pinpoint the possible locations of the marine foundations; providing the underwater concrete through the Pre-Pakt method; securing living quarters for key personnel; and arranging for the largest armada of construction vessels ever assembled for peacetime purposes.

Orders were placed on the books of the American Bridge Division at its Ambridge, Pennsylvania, plant to roll, fabricate, and lay out the towers and the truss spans for the more than four miles of over-the-water crossing. A subcontract was let to the Roebling Cable and Wire Company in Trenton, New Jersey, for the 33,000 miles of steel wire about the thickness of a pencil that would eventually be bound together to make up the two 24.25-inch-in-diameter cables that would hold up the center and side spans.

These were exciting days, and the residents of the Straits area freeing themselves of winter's grip began with great gusto to plan the groundbreaking ceremonies on both

114

sides of the Straits. Platforms were erected at the precise spot of each projected bridge head. Red, white, and blue bunting was literally draped all over both towns. High school bands from the bridgehead and surrounding cities rehearsed diligently for the celebration, which came off with flying colors over a two-day period, May 7 in St. Ignace and May 8 in Mackinaw City.

On the first day of the festivities, politicians from the governor on down spoke glowingly of this groundbreaking as a milestone in Michigan's history—which indeed it was. Even the politicians who had opposed the bridge jumped on the bandwagon, and there was room for all to bask in the glory of the accomplishment—to date. The only dampening occurrence was perpetrated by Mother Nature, who dumped eleven inches of wet snow in the area surrounding St. Ignace and more than an inch on the groundbreaking site. It was cold and damp. When I left Lansing the day before, the temperature was in the sixties, and I had no topcoat or rain gear. Fortunately, I was able to borrow a slightly soiled, white, down-filled jacket which I wore during the ceremony. If I wasn't the best-dressed person at this important celebration, I did at least stave off pneumonia!

The next day, similar groundbreaking events were held in Mackinaw City. The weather was more cooperative and as a result the speeches were a bit longer, but nobody really seemed to mind. Mrs. Brown and Mrs. Fisher, equipped with white-handled, chromium-plated shovels, dug daintily into the ground and dutifully did it over and over again for photographers, who competed vigorously to capture this precious moment in Michigan history.

Meanwhile, squads of engineers under the guidance of Steinman's immediate subordinates in New York were furiously working on the hundreds of detailed design drawings needed for the contractors to begin construction as soon as possible. Months of work were compressed into weeks. The public views progress on a construction project by what can be seen. Little does it realize that before anything viewable can happen, a plan has to be followed. In the case of the

Mackinac Bridge, plans sufficient only for bidding purposes were prepared. It was only after February 17, 1954, when the funds were in hand, that Steinman could give the go-ahead signal on detailed drawings, and then it became a race for his staff to stay ahead of the contractors. Every bit of earth removed or filled in, above or below the surface, had to be described in detailed drawings that the contractors could follow. Every piece of steel that was cut, riveted, or bolted had to be shown. Every cubic yard of concrete had a precise location in which it had to be placed. Everything had to meet agreed-upon specifications. Thus, everything done was inspected and tested.

Nowhere was this more dramatically illustrated than in connection with the locations of the foundations, the underwater structures. Soundings of the Straits bottom had been made along the proposed line of the bridge during the late 1930s. They revealed a deep gorge in the center of the Straits. There was no reliable information on the underlying rock. Thus, the two priority procedures were, first, to bore into the rock to determine its character, its depth, and its contour; and second, to survey the line of bridge and the proposed location of the foundations. These tests commenced even before groundbreaking, and their results presented the engineers and the Authority with their first major decision.

The problem arose in connection with the location of the north tower foundation. The borings into the rock on the planned location for the foundation revealed a peculiar formation: it was at a point where the rock bottom sloped gently toward the middle of the Straits except that, by sheer coincidence, where the 135-foot-in-diameter foundation for the north tower would come to rest on the bottom, there was a steep hump on the down side of the slope. If the weight of the foundation were placed on this hump, there was a danger of its breaking off. The foundation would then go with it. If an attempt were made to level it with underwater explosives, there was the risk of making the slope sharper and totally unsuitable for a foundation base. So what to do?

Move all thirty-three foundations 30 feet north! Thus

Pier 1, which had been shown on the bid drawings on the shore in Mackinaw City where the Department of Natural Resources Orientation Center now stands, is in the water just north of the building.

Pier 19, the north tower foundation, was moved 30 feet north and sunk to rock bottom on a relatively level location 210 feet below the surface; Pier 33, which was to have been built in the water about 25 feet south of the causeway, ended up being sunk through the causeway to rock. Of course, the remaining thirty foundations were also moved, but since construction had not commenced, it was what one might term a paper decision.

18

A Huff and a Puff Was Not Enough

November 1, 1957, the date the bridge was scheduled to be opened for traffic, was only a few months away. The members of the Authority, meeting on June 7, 1957, were elated that the target date set four years earlier would be met. It was indeed a remarkable achievement in the annals of major construction projects, especially because it was a large bridge and because of the limited construction season and the violent storms for which the Straits of Mackinac is notorious. It was a great tribute to the competence and experience of the consulting engineers and the two major contractors.

The measure of the skill and efficiency of contractors is not, in my opinion, so much in their ability to build when all goes well. There are many contractors who could have built several parts of the Mackinac Bridge providing no problems arose, but the real test and talent of the contractor comes into play when something goes wrong. The first and perhaps most important thing is to recognize a problem when it arises. This involves a readiness to realize that additional cost and delay may occur. Some contractors shudder at these possibilities and make an effort to cover the error. Sometimes they get away with it. More often they do not. Second, a responsible and experienced contractor will take immediate steps to solve a problem or correct an error. Often, there may occur a three-sided discussion as to the blame for a problem among the designer, the owner, and the contractor. But action comes first: solve the problem, correct the error, tear out work done if it's not right, and do it over until it is right. Then argue about the blame. That is the way it was during the Mackinac Bridge construction. While the bridge was being built, there were accidents, delays, and arguments over the meaning of specifications. In a project so vast, there were bound to be areas that were not clearly covered. For example, when the deck contractor pours concrete and some of it drips on the steel below, who cleans it? And how? Just hose it off as it lands, or wait because the superstructure contractor, who has not fully bolted the steel, does not want any hosing done while his men are working? By the time he finishes, the concrete is hardened, and the cost of removal increases.

This is but one example of the scores of confrontations faced by the contractors vis-à-vis another contractor, the Authority, and the consulting engineer on an almost daily basis. Both brief and lengthy discussions ensued. Both quick and prolonged settlements were reached. Every effort to avoid being disagreeable was made on all sides when disagreement occurred. Though tempers flared occasionally, the work went on. Work stoppages are the bane of construction efficiency. They hurt all parties: the worker, who does not get paid; the contractor, whose equipment stands idle; the owner, who is paying interest on borrowed money; and, last but not least, the public, who ultimately pays for any additional costs and is delayed in the use of the facility.

Notwithstanding the immensity of the project and the involvement of twenty prime contractors and a host of subcontractors, only one threatened legal action developed and that was ultimately settled out of court. During the consulting engineer's annual inspection in the summer of 1958, he noticed that the one-hundred-foot-long steel sheets driven to refusal around the underwater frame for Pier 17, the south anchor block, were coming loose. By summer's end, the sheets on the west and part of the north sides had actually torn loose from their bolts and fallen over into the Straits. There was no immediate danger to the foundation, but it could not be left that way. The consulting engineer promptly provided plans for removing the bent sheets and replacing them with new ones and at the same time adding three additional feet of concrete and steel in the areas affected. Bids were taken, a contract awarded, and the work done. The Authority sued the substructure contractor for the amount of the extra work, $422,000. The suit was resisted, but a few weeks before going to trial a settlement was reached. The Authority and the contractors split the cost. This was considered fair on the rationale that the Authority got an additional three feet of foundation and the contractor paid for the removal of the bent sheets.

It is interesting to note that the bridge construction was not certified as complete until December 31, 1963, six years after it was opened. There were several reasons for the time lapse: work considered complete by a contractor was challenged by the consulting engineer; minor defects developed and had to be remedied. All such matters had to be discussed, responsibilities determined, and costs negotiated, until matters were finally settled. The amount of extras paid to contractors was truly insignificant compared to the total bridge cost. When the construction was certified as complete, the Authority still had $236,000 in its construction fund, which was established six months before work on the bridge began.

It would be misleading not to acknowledge the fact that there is a certain amount of luck involved in the completion of such a large project without some serious and costly delay. There could have been storms that would have destroyed partially completed work. Of course the contractors took steps to anticipate such events, but still they do happen, as they did several times during the construction of the Golden Gate Bridge. One such protective measure comes to mind because it nearly led to my severance from the Authority. As the first construction season was coming to a close in December 1954, the caissons, or forms, for the foundations that would hold the main towers had not been sunk all the way down to rock bottom. Visualize a circular double-walled steel can 135 feet in diameter and about 175 feet high with its bottom third penetrating the overburden, the mud and loose stones lying above the rock, and its empty top two-thirds in water. Bear in mind that windrows of ice (ice piled on top of ice up to twenty feet high) are being blown back and forth through the Straits all winter long. The ice pressure on the empty can would be terrific. To offset this pressure and keep the caisson upright, the contractor decided to bring in several shiploads of rock to be dumped all around the caisson above the overburden. This would counteract the ice pressure at the surface and secure the caisson.

Pursuant to the terms and specifications of the contract with Merritt-Chapman & Scott, the safety and protection of the work accomplished rested with that firm. The extra precaution they took to protect the caisson was their own decision and at their own expense, as were many others during the course of construction. The rock dumping procedure was not at the expense of the Authority. Consequently, I was not immediately aware that it was being done. At the time my office was still in Lansing.

Somehow, the soon-to-be-defunct *Detroit Times* got wind of this precautionary measure and came out with a headline that the Mackinac Bridge foundations were "dangling in the ice" and in danger of being knocked over by the forthcoming winter's ice. The late Frank Morris, a highly imaginative journalist who at the time was the paper's political correspondent in Lansing, had a field day speculating on how the bridge piers, like so many duckpins (or was it dominoes?), would be toppled by the mountainous windrows that moved glacier-like through the Straits. He also drew a parallel between Bridge Authority Chairman Prentiss M. Brown trying to hold back the ice and King Canute trying to keep back the tide. Of course, Morris did mention that the contractors

121

were "desperately" unloading rock around the main tower foundations in an effort to save them from disaster. The thrust and character of the story were a hairline this side of doomsday, disclosing that the nation's foremost engineers were praying for mild weather.

I was assigned to correct Morris. It turned out to be a futile effort. Anything I said sounded as though I were confirming his conclusion. Furthermore, he would not divulge who gave him his information. Thus, I could not get a statement from the source denying any danger. Brown's wire to the paper, attempting to reassure the public and stating that the story was based on a ridiculous rumor, was made to appear self-serving. The chairman was quite unhappy with me—in fact he was furious—because I was away when the story broke and left again after I thought I had a promise from Morris that he would print a complete explanation, if not a retraction. I got neither, but I did get a handwritten, rather severe reprimand from Prentiss Brown.

Nothing happened to the foundations, because the contractor had taken the necessary precaution of stabilizing them inside and out with shiploads of stone. I became almost paranoid in my suspicions of many persons who might have tipped off Morris about the need for the rock. I blush now when I think of all the innocent people I suspected. Several years later, I concluded that it was an ambitious public relations man for the company which had supplied the stone. His motivation, I thought, was to inform the public that his client had a hand in building the great Mackinac Bridge. But I was wrong. Prentiss Brown wrote in his diary, on December 6, 1954, that "F. Morris called and was apologetic and said it came thru Gillis of Times who got story from ferry offices."

Don Gillis, outdoor editor of the *Detroit Times*, was visiting with ferryboat officers while crossing the Straits. They apparently told him they had seen shiploads of rock being dumped around the foundations. Most of the ferry personnel, for good reason, were opposed to the bridge and might have speculated aloud that the rock was being dumped because the foundations would never withstand the ice pressure. That was all the reporters needed; they were off and running.

This incident is important for several reasons, the least of which is that I almost got fired. Mainly, it illustrates that good contractors anticipate problems and take steps to avoid them, even if their doing so inadvertently leads to some negative publicity.

During the same construction season, another crisis occurred. Had there been an alert press in the area, it would have had a field day. Commencing October 31, 1954, and for nearly a week, the resident engineer's daily construction report contained an alarming remark concerning Pier 18, the cable bent foundation just north of the south anchor block: "Caisson is now leaning slightly north and west."

No measurements of the list are noted, but the word "leaning" is enough to raise the eyebrows of even the coolest of marine foundation contractors. The next day's report stated that the caisson had "resumed vertical movement," but this did not last long. On Tuesday, November 2, the engineer noted, "Caisson leaning north and west. Excavating in south wells to correct list. Caisson resumed movement. C. E. at minus 125 feet. List .37 W., 1.27 N."

Translated, this laconic report says that the bottom of the cutting edge ("C. E.") of the caisson, a 92-by-44-foot steel box into which concrete would be poured, had reached a depth of 125 feet. Excavation was taking place on the south side of the caisson to make it easier for the bottom to cut deeper on that side. Hopefully this would level the caisson which was leaning 1.27 feet, or about 16 inches, north. The next day the lean to the north became more pronounced, more than a foot and a half despite the previous day's corrective action. This would certainly make a bridge builder's heart skip a beat, especially when accompanied by the report that the "lake became very rough in evening, southwest wind at 35 miles per hour at 1900 hours. Work on night shift about stopped by rough seas . . . list increasing."

The next day, the report indicates a lengthy discussion

between Steinman's resident engineer, Jack Kinney, and Merritt-Chapman & Scott's project manager, Grover Denny. The calm, deliberate language of the report explaining the condition of the caisson and what they intended to do about it belies the urgency of the situation. I am confident that had a reporter been present at the discussion, the lead paragraph in his story would have disclosed that the foundation was in imminent danger of falling over.

The next day's report stated that "work greatly held up by weather" but that there was a slight improvement in the list. More improvement followed the next day. Gradually the list subsided. The cutting edge reached rock bottom, and the entire caisson was subsequently filled with concrete. The incident in the eyes of experienced bridge builders could be considered routine because they knew how to avert disaster. But had there been a long and continuous stretch of stormy weather at the Straits, they might not have been so fortunate. At the risk of arousing some criticism among contractors and engineers, I would conclude that luck plays a fair role in the successful conclusion of many construction projects.

Came the Day!

Came the Day! November 1, 1957. The deadline was met as it was precisely scheduled by Steinman, carried out by the contractors, and overseen by the Authority. The media had a field day. The press lavished praise. It was refreshing to read front-page upbeat headlines and news stories. If any dark thoughts surfaced, they may have been due to petty jealousies aroused by someone getting a little more ink or credit than deserved. But meeting this deadline was not easy and two problems did arise—or more accurately, one problem and one big question.

The public did not realize that the bridge might not have been opened for traffic on November 1, 1957. During the fall of that year the American Bridge Division had to weld hundreds of sections of the steel grid surface of the main span to the supporting crossbeams of the deck. It was a labor-intensive, tedious, time-consuming job requiring literally tens of thousands of spot welds by scores of welders. Bad weather during September and October had limited working hours and the deck installation had fallen behind schedule. The contractors informed us that they might not be able to complete the grid deck and that the opening of the bridge might have to be delayed. I knew they were asking for time because they did not want to increase their payroll to hire extra help or pay for overtime by their current work force.

I explained to them that the invitations for the bridge opening on November 1 had already been printed; that the media had been alerted; that VIPs had been scheduled to appear; and that the bridge opening would take place on November 1, with or without the grid. If we had to raid every lumber yard around to lay wooden planks on the cross-beams, we would do it.

With that the meeting broke up. I can only imagine what went on among the superstructure contractor's personnel: was I bluffing about the planks? If not, it certainly would be embarrassing to answer media questions about a wooden deck where there should have been steel. How much was involved in overtime or additional personnel to meet the target date? I daresay some long distance calls were made between St. Ignace and company headquarters in Pittsburgh. But when November 1 came around, the deck was done. How? A little overtime, a little more help, and an improvement in the weather.

Then came the question of the opening ceremonies.

November normally is not conducive to such outdoor events as dedications or parades. Football and hunting are fine, but standing around at the Straits of Mackinac or out on the bridge listening to speeches could be a bit much. So the Authority accepted my suggestion that the opening ceremonies be confined to a press or media tour with invitations also sent to state officers and legislators, engineers, contractors, and other persons directly concerned with the project. Then, in June of the following year when the Straits area is usually blessed with sunshine and flowers, a gala four-day celebration could be conducted, climaxed by the dedication of the bridge.

November 1, 1957, was as fickle as November 12, 13, and 14, 1952, when the underwriters were trying to impress possible bond purchasers with the long lineup of hunter traffic only to be betrayed by one of the mildest Indian summers in memory, which made it possible for the ferries sailing on the glassy Straits to keep up with the traffic. Five years later, we again were surprised by mild weather, which was delightful for the opening day ceremonies. But this caused another problem: persons from the Straits area who normally would not have left their homes for an outdoor event in November came flocking to the Straits by the hundreds to participate in the opening of the Mackinac Bridge. The residents of Mackinaw City had graciously laid out a buffet for the three hundred invited guests. More than double showed up. But Mackinaw City hosts and hostesses made do. After the last person at that luncheon was served, there was not a cold cut or loaf of bread to be found anywhere in the Lower Peninsula within fifteen miles of the Straits.

The press busses drove out onto the center of the bridge at 10:00 A.M. as scheduled. The Authority members occupied a custom-built Chrysler open parade car, which I drove. We were followed by the VIPs and the not-so-important people, some of whom took enraged exception with me for my not having sent them invitations. The monumental importance of the occasion, however, quickly dissipated any confrontations, and all who came were welcome.

There were no speeches. Governor Williams made some informal remarks addressed primarily to the media people. He presented cuff links adorned with the state seal to members of the Authority and a few others. He also distributed souvenir ceramic plates and ashtrays. I got the ceramics, not the cuff links. Dr. Steinman also spoke briefly and mentioned again the aerodynamic stability of the bridge, one of his favorite features of the design. The press never accurately explained what he meant. Steinman described in detail the wind tunnel tests he had made of a scaled-down section of the Mackinac Bridge at the University of Oregon Engineering Laboratory. Since the collapse of the Tacoma Narrows Bridge in 1940, extensive research had been conducted to determine the cause of its failure. The laboratory tested the proposed designs for new structures to determine their aerodynamic stability.

The Tacoma Narrows Bridge succumbed to winds with a velocity of only 42 miles per hour, which is relatively mild and just a little above normal at the Straits during the fall of the year. The reason for the failure was inherent in the design. The stiffening trusses or vertical beams on each side of the deck were solid and eight feet in height. When struck by wind from a certain direction, they reacted like the leading edge of an airplane wing, causing the solid surface deck to rise and fall. Gradually, the structure absorbed energy from the wind. In doing so, the distortion of the deck increased, as did its rising and falling, until the bridge twisted itself to destruction.

The researchers at the laboratory tested Steinman's section and by extrapolation concluded that it showed no aerodynamic instability no matter what the velocity of the wind. Theoretically, it would not twist itself to destruction because of its inherent design, even in winds of infinite velocity. Steinman tried to explain this in simple terms. He was careful to point out that the steel trusses were designed to withstand pressure of 50 pounds per square foot, or a wind velocity of 125 miles per hour. But most reporters seized upon the "infinite velocity" expression to dramatize Steinman's statement. They wrote that the Mackinac Bridge could withstand whatever winds might blow.

That must have raised some eyebrows in engineering and meteorological circles. Anybody who has ever witnessed or been in a tornado, which means winds of 200 to 250 miles per hour, knows that nothing stays put. Fortunately, the Straits of Mackinac is not in tornado country, but if there were winds of "infinite velocity" blowing through the Straits, the bridge would be somewhere around Mackinac Island, but who knows where Mackinac Island would be?

There was no wind at all at the Straits on November 1, 1957, until about four o'clock in the afternoon. With all the posing, picture taking, and tape recording completed and the lunch in Mackinaw City consumed, the schedule called for the return trip northbound with Governor Williams paying the first bridge toll to Prentiss M. Brown. Once again we got into the Chrysler parade car and this time it was agreed that Governor Williams would drive. But, unfortunately, he had let his driver's license expire. He really had no occasion to drive; governors rarely do. So Nancy Williams took the wheel and in those pre-ERA days, it raised a few eyebrows.

Pursuant to the plan, Brown donned a fare collector's cap. Governor Williams handed him his check for $3.25 to dramatize the fact that there was no free passage, not even for governors, for those crossing the Mackinac Bridge. Of course, checks are not accepted either, but the governor never told me he was going to use a check, and it was too late to invoke the rule. Williams knew well that everybody must pay to cross the bridge. Several years later, the governor was hosting John F. Kennedy, then a candidate for president, on a trip to the Upper Peninsula. There were four cars in the party which had stopped at one of the anchor blocks for pictures. The governor was in the lead car when they arrived at the fare booths. Somehow a car that was not part of the official entourage got in among those that were. The governor, always the soul of graciousness, paid for five cars and left a curious bridge crosser wondering why the fare collector would not accept his money.

The first official car, the first official payee, and the first official bridge-crosser ceremony went off without a hitch. However, when it came to first among the general public, there were many claims for this honor, and they may be valid but not official. Al Carter, a jazz band drummer from Chicago who made a hobby of being "first" at various events, had been in line since the night before the opening in order to be first across the bridge. As soon as the governor paid his fare the signal was given for the fare booths to open, and Carter made his famous dash to be first, and he was so proclaimed by the press. The car he used is now in the Grand Rapids Historical Museum.

Within a week after the opening, the bridge got its first test of Mackinac Straits winds and its first encounter with lightweight trailers, which would gently blow over on their sides. It was embarrassing, and very soon the buddy system was established. Drivers of trucks and other heavily loaded, solid vehicles were requested to escort the lightweight vehicles by driving on the windward side of them. This system was nearly 100 percent perfect, and after its inauguration the only times vehicles turned over was either when the wind came up so suddenly that there was no time to invoke the procedure or when some impatient driver outran his escort.

There was, however, one incident that bears retelling. On November 10, 1975—the same day the ore carrier *Edmund Fitzgerald* broke up and sank in a storm on Lake Superior with the loss of thirty-two lives—the buddy system had been operating at the bridge for southbound vehicles since about 1:00 P.M. The winds out of the west increased as the afternoon wore on. At about 3:00 P.M., an Authority patrol car radioed that a southbound tractor-trailer combination, an escort vehicle, had toppled over onto the compact car it was escorting at Pier 17, the south anchor block and the scene of most wind accidents. I inquired if anybody were hurt, and the report came back that the driver of the semitrailer complained of injury. Instructions were given to get him to the nearest hospital, in St. Ignace, but he would not go back across the bridge, so he was taken to Cheboygan. Chief Engineer Orlando Doyle and I went out to assess the situation. The tractor trailer had flattened the compact car, but the owner of that car miraculously had escaped injury. His only concern was for his dog, which was retrieved for him unharmed by bridge personnel. The wind-toppled vehicle had fallen across the pavement, blocking all lanes so that traffic could not move in either direction. In a few minutes wreckers were on the scene intent upon clearing at least one and possibly two lanes, but by this time the wind velocity had increased to gusts of up to ninety miles per hour. The men could not stand upright. Walking bent over or on their hands and knees was too dangerous for the work to be done. The

130

accident held up traffic for more than four hours until the wind subsided. One lane in each direction was then opened. It was the worst wind experienced at the bridge, which of course sustained no damage.

The driver of the southbound tractor-trailer combination who agreed to be an escort when he paid his fare was not asked and did not reveal that his trailer was empty. But because it was empty, the updraft at Pier 17 in those record-high winds was enough to topple his trailer, which in turn pulled over his tractor. His injuries were not too serious, but he nevertheless decided to sue the Authority in the State Court of Claims. His wife also sued the Authority for lack of consortium. Several weeks later at a meeting of the Authority, I reported the incident and the two law suits.

Former governor Murray D. Van Wagoner, then seventy-six years old, vice-chairman of the Authority, and known for speaking his mind and his detestation of big words, wanted to know what "lack of consortium" was. When it was explained to him, he said, "Hell, give her my phone number!" Both law suits, however, were withdrawn.

What They Wrought

The Ultimate Cost

During more than twenty-five years and approximately 1,500 public discussions about the Mackinac Bridge, I am asked a variety of questions, but very often the first one asked is, "How many people were killed during the bridge's construction?" It makes no difference whether the audience is male or female, old or young, white-collar or blue-collar, I can always depend on the fatality question. A classic experience comes to mind. For more than ten years a suburban Detroit school with a children's camp forty miles south of the Straits bussed its students, from five to ten years of age, to the bridge for an inspection tour and a discussion with me. Every year there were new students, but there were always two characteristics of the annual session that stayed the same: one, the depth and soundness of the questions asked and, two, the curiosity about the fatalities. They wanted all the details surrounding the loss of five lives during the bridge construction. I assume the readers of this book are likewise interested.

The first death occurred on September 10, 1954, when Frank Pepper, a hard-hat diver (he dove in a brass helmet and compressed-air suit) with more than twenty years of experience, was inspecting Pier 19, the south main tower foundation, for Merritt-Chapman & Scott. He had been underwater at about 140 to 150 feet for nearly an hour when he signaled to his tender that he wanted to come up at once because he was cold. As an experienced diver, he knew not to surface too quickly, but he did so this time. He was supposedly cautioned about his fast rise, but he chose to disdain the advice. He contracted the bends, or the diver's disease. Pepper was promptly carried to a decompression chamber accompanied by five bridge workers to aid him. The doctor was called, but Pepper died before his arrival.

The next death was James R. Le Sarge, another Merritt-Chapman & Scott employee. The twenty-six-year-old was working on Pier 20, the foundation for the north main tower, on October 10, 1954, when he fell inside the reinforced steel form. It was a forty-foot drop into the caisson, and his head struck several steel braces during the fall. He was probably dead before he hit the bottom.

The third fatality was a strange occurrence. Forty-year-old Albert B. Abbott, of St. Ignace, was not considered an agile climber by his colleagues, but that made no difference because he was working on the foundations and did not need to climb. One day while walking on a beam eighteen inches wide and not more than four feet above the water, he fell in. His co-workers thought he had tripped or misstepped and would surface momentarily. He did not. They went in after him, but by the time his body was recovered it was too late. These three lives were lost within a forty-day period during this first construction season.

Stories are told about bodies being buried in massive concrete structures such as bridge foundations, but they are 99 percent untrue. There is, however, one bridge worker on the bottom of the Straits, but not in concrete. Twenty-eight-year-old Jack C. Baker of Pagosa Springs, Colorado, and twenty-seven-year-old Robert Koppen of Plymouth, Michigan, spent their first day on the job for American Bridge Division at the top of the 552-foot-high north tower, where they were placing the chain link fence that would be used by the cable spinners. The chain link fence, or spinners' platform, was attached to 8-by-10-inch, 10-foot-long wooden ties. These, in turn, were attached to five 2.5-inch-in-diameter wire ropes stretching 8,614 feet—the full length of the total suspension—from anchor block to anchor block. The wire ropes followed the curvature that the cable would take and the flexible chain link fence would provide the underfoot area on which the men handling the 12,580 pencil-thick wires would stand, walk around, and get to and from their work stations.

The procedure for placing the platform was to raise bundles of the chain link fence, which were folded up like maps, to the tower top. Ties on the bundles would then be attached to the wire ropes with U-shaped brackets so that the packages could slide down the wire ropes as they were unfolded. A restraining line held the packages in place in order to control the speed at which they would unfold and slide down the supporting ropes. Baker, Koppen, Robert Anderson, who was in charge, and Louis Stepman, his assistant, were assigned to stand at the top of the tower to push a package with their feet to help gravity make the chain link fence unfold. The restraining line broke and the entire package, about 100 feet long, went careening down the wire ropes like an uncontrolled roller coaster. Baker and Koppen were caught in this plunging mass of fence and thrown into the Straits from a height of 550 feet.

Stepman and Anderson hung on for their lives.

Anderson, badly bruised, with a broken ankle, was on top of the fence when it came to a halt. Stepman, below him, was hanging by his fingers to a vertical portion of the fence that had broken away from the wire ropes. He shouted up to Anderson his intention to let go. It would have been a drop of about 400 feet into the Straits. Anderson ordered him to hang on and to try to climb up the wire fence to where he was. Stepman kicked off his shoes, and getting a toehold in the fence links, was able to make it to safety. Had he dropped into the Straits, he surely would have died.

Baker's body, which did not sink, was immediately recovered. Work was suspended, and a three-day search for Koppen was begun with boats and divers. It was a costly and fruitless effort. The currents at the bottom of the Straits are unpredictable, the water always cold. The Straits rarely gives up its dead.

The names of all of these five men who lost their lives during the bridge construction are engraved on a bronze plaque on the west side of Pier 1 in Mackinaw City. The plaque was erected by the Michigan Building and Trades Council and dedicated on November 1, 1957, the day the bridge was opened.

There is a rule of thumb among high-level construction workers that a life is lost for every ten million dollars spent on a project. It is without basis. Safety devices, education, and legal requirements are reducing the risks with every new project undertaken. The American Bridge Division, a leader in safety precautions, had several employees on the bridge whose exclusive duties were to constantly watch for and protect workers from dangerous situations. One of these workers was somewhat of a male chauvinist. Women visitors were not permitted on this contractor's area of work for fear they would distract the male employees, for whom one misstep could spell death. The presence of a woman might turn a man's head when his eyes should be fixed on a narrow beam 200 feet above the water or watching for a red-hot rivet that his partner is tossing to him some 30 or 40 feet away.

There was also the possibility of a liability claim if a woman wearing an open-toe shoe or high heels injured herself among the bolts, tools, and chunks of steel that get strewn on areas where people could be walking. So it was that during the building of the superstructure, only male visitors were accommodated. Of course, there had to be a good reason for any visit.

However, an unusual incident occurred toward the end of construction. American Bridge's head safety inspector had reached the age of retirement. One day after office hours the staff, including several wives and female secretaries, had a little party for him, at the conclusion of which he invited all present, including the secretaries and wives, to a trip out on the bridge. Perhaps it was his way of saying at long last what he thought about the restriction of female visitors.

21

One Picture Equals a Thousand Memories

Even before the $96,400,033.33 check was handed over to the Authority, history-minded Prentiss M. Brown and your publicity-minded author were thinking about the necessity for making a photographic record of all the important events related to the proposed structure from the receipt of the funds to the day of dedication. This thinking was given impetus by the offers of several reputable photographers and photographic concerns to be responsible for the pictorial history of the Mackinac Bridge.

Also, the American Bridge Division, Merritt-Chapman & Scott, and David B. Steinman had made it clear that they wanted movies as well as still photos for their files and publicity. Of course, there would also be requests from newspapers, wire services, magazines, television stations, and advertising agencies for photographs and film footage. The general public, too, would want the opportunity to record the building of the "impossible bridge."

It did not take much imagination to visualize the confusion that would arise out of all these demands. Because construction was taking place in the Straits, water transport would be needed to photograph the action. On a sunny day suitable for photography or on a day when some vital part of the construction would be performed, there would be a clamor for boats, escorts, engineers, and whatever other assistance photographers and cinematographers would require. It would present a big problem for all concerned.

The contractors' public relations personnel were invited to a meeting to discuss the problem and listen to a proposed solution. Several subcontractors, notably the Pre-Pakt Concrete Company, were also concerned. It was proposed that the Authority hire a photographer who was skillful with both still and movie cameras and could develop and print his own photographs. It was further proposed that when necessary an assistant would be placed on the Authority payroll. These persons would supply all parties with all the photographs and movie film they needed for files, publicity, advertising, whatever. In return the contractors would build a darkroom and purchase the photographic equipment and supplies.

At first, there was some opposition to forfeiting 100 percent control over photography to an Authority-operated and -administered program, but when they began to evaluate the practical advantages of the idea, it became more palatable. For example, suppose Merritt-Chapman & Scott wanted a film record of placing the first foundation form in the Straits. The company could schedule it a week in advance and send out a photographer from New York, Chicago, or Detroit to get the picture. Of course, he or she would be unfamiliar with the operation. A boat, and someone to explain what was going on, would be needed, and there could be inclement weather so that the entire operation would be delayed until it cleared. By then, the cost of the coverage would have been prohibitive to the public relations people.

Confronted by this sort of scenario, the participants in the meeting began to see the wisdom of having a photographer on the site who would understand the construction procedures, be on a first-name basis with all the key personnel, and be available whenever any important construction event took place. In addition, the photographer would escort any photographers, either working for an accredited publication or free-lance, seeking their own special film coverage of the project.

Though the public relations people had some reservations (as did I, the author of the plan), they agreed—at least on a trial basis. Thus, prior to the groundbreaking I interviewed a dozen or so applicants for the position of "official bridge photographer." I suggested to the ones whose accomplishments and personalities met my standards that they photograph the groundbreaking ceremonies and show me their results. Because this was to be done at their own expense, it reduced the number of applicants, but did have the effect of screening out persons who were not overly enthusiastic about the importance of the Mackinac Bridge and therefore not the best candidates for its publicity. It should be kept in mind that there was still a large percentage of Michigan residents who either did not care a whit about a permanent link at the Straits of Mackinac or did not think it could be built.

The Authority was very lucky. Herman Ellis, a teacher by education, a photographer by profession, a travel lecturer by avocation, and a gentleman by every definition, photographed the groundbreaking ceremonies and provided us with both stills and movies. Immediately upon seeing the results, we hired him. During his tenure, he took literally thousands of black-and-white and color pictures, along with tens of thousands of feet of 16-mm color film of bridge construction, fulfilling the needs of the Authority, the consulting engineer, the two main contractors, one subcontractor, and untold numbers of newspapers, wire services, magazines, advertising agencies, educational institutions, and private individuals.

He supplied the basic photography for three twenty-eight-minute 16-mm color sound films: "Mackinac Bridge Diary" for the American Bridge Division; "Getting a Toehold in the Straits" for Merritt-Chapman & Scott; and a promotional film for the Pre-Pakt Concrete Company. Thousands of additional feet of film were sent to television station producers for use in newscasts as well as in special features.

During the height of the construction Ellis had two assistants: Mickey Duggan, a skillful and resourceful photographer, and after his departure, Harold Bell, another expert with a camera, both daring and imaginative.

Ellis was the antithesis of the stereotypical news photographer. He was the soul of courtesy and would no more order anybody, sultan or servant, to "move over" than he would jump off the bridge. But he always managed to get his picture. He was anything but a lithe, athletic man; indeed, he was a bit paunchy, and his round face further emphasized his girth, but when I asked him if he would climb out on the bridge during construction, he assured me it would be no problem. One of his prize-winning pictures shows two steel workers standing on separated parts of the chain link fence platform to be used for cable spinning when it was about to be joined at the bottom of the center span 150 feet above the Straits. The men are reaching toward each other to join hands, the first to do so on a permanent link over the Straits. The photo was taken from the same height about 50 feet away. Let the reader speculate on what held up the photographer.

Upon completion of bridge construction, Ellis would take leaves of absence to make travel pictures of Michigan, the Midwest, Arizona, and Africa. He became one of the stars of the travel lecture series and was on tour all over the United States. He also appeared regularly on television. His title as official photographer for the Mackinac Bridge brought the project to the attentions of thousands of persons who might otherwise never have heard of the Straits of Mackinac.

Ellis had many interesting experiences with some of the country's foremost photographers. *National Geographic*, *Life*, and *Look*, picture magazines with circulations in the millions, dispatched their ace photographers to the Straits. One of them, Margaret Bourke-White, perhaps the most famous feature photographer of the period, informed Ellis that she would be at the Straits on or about a certain date. It was understood that because of her prestige and reputation, he and a boat and whatever else was necessary would be available when and if she arrived. Ellis in turn notified Prentiss M. Brown just in case he cared to meet the distinguished woman. He indicated that he had seen her around the nation's capital once or twice during his congressional career.

She came unannounced. Ellis scrambled to get everything arranged and put in a call to Brown that Bourke-White had arrived and that they would be departing the Merritt-Chapman & Scott dock shortly should he wish to go along. He did, but it seems that he had had some dental work done a day or two before and was without his dentures; also, being retired he saw no need to shave every morning or perhaps two mornings if he were not going out. Everybody around town knew "P.M.," and he fit into the community like an old shoe. He would not hesitate to be seen by his neighbors in a shawl collar cardigan of the 1920s vintage or an uncreased pair of trousers and visored cloth cap. He was dressed thus when he joined Ellis and the great photographer. Ellis later related that he introduced Bourke-White and Brown amid the casting off of lines and the revving up of the motor. He was never sure if she heard that he was chairman of the Authority, but he was sure that she treated him as though he were some local character who just came along for the ride. All the time they were out on the Straits she completely ignored him, and he her. Finally, when they were docking the ice broke and the two became very chummy, exchanging pleasantries and engaging in animated conversation. Ellis never knew whether Bourke-White did not know Brown was a former U.S. senator until the assignment was practically over, or whether she was so deeply engrossed in what she was doing that she did not care.

Ellis died in 1975, but his work never will. His bridge photos still appear on walls, in publications, wherever people will see them. "Mackinac Bridge Diary," for which he did the photography, is still in demand and being shown on television and in school auditoriums and service clubs throughout the Midwest. The plan for providing interested parties with bridge pictures was unique, but Ellis made it work. He was a great photographer and a fine person.

22

Green and White, Maize and Blue

Michigan State University fans point with pride to the ivory towers and green truss spans of the Mackinac Bridge. But it was only by coincidence that the bridge colors resemble the Spartans' green and white.

Loyal University of Michigan fans have something to cheer about in the bridge lighting. The ninety-six globes along the cables are amber, while the mercury-vapor lights on the bridge road or deck cast off a bluish hue. Was this the result of a University of Michigan alumnus with an influential connection? Let it be said that the lighting color scheme was less by coincidence than design.

Shortly after the bridge financing was completed and the contingency construction contracts were implemented, Merritt-Chapman & Scott started ordering boats and seagoing equipment that would be used in the bridge construction. In April 1954, I received a phone call from an advertising agency.

"What color or colors will the bridge be painted?" inquired a representative of the agency's art department.

"Why do you ask?" I wanted to know.

"We're preparing some layouts for Chrysler Marine.

Their engines will be used in the equipment to build the Mackinac Bridge, and our client wants to advertise the fact."

"That's great, but I can't be of much help. The color scheme hasn't been selected. The only thing I can tell you is that it won't be black or gray."

Traditionally, steel bridges and other structures exposed to the atmosphere had been painted gray or black. These two paint colors provided the best protection against the ravages of the weather (sun, rain, temperature extremes) and salt water; but, as post-World War II paints improved in their durability against weathering, the range of colors that would provide protection increased. Steinman was one of the first bridge designers to recommend that his structures be painted colors other than gray or black.

My curiosity about how the advertising agency would depict the bridge was satisfied several months later. I had been told that the ad would appear in *Fortune* and other leading business publications, and it did run in the July 1954 issue of *Fortune*. The ad pictured the magnificent Mackinac Bridge arising out of the stormy Straits, its towers soaring skyward in beautiful ivory to touch fleecy white clouds bathed in blue. The sturdy steel trusses of foliage green spanned the turbulent waters, exuding strength and action, which the artist obviously wanted the viewer to associate with the industrial marine engines being advertised. When the members of the Authority and the consulting engineers saw the ad, they decided on those bridge colors. We never did find out if the artist was a Michigan State University alumnus or fan. Nor did we attempt to establish his identity—until this chapter was being written. The best I could do then was to find the artist's signature on his painting reproduced in the ad. It was understandably difficult to read, and the most I could make of it was "Steven Baragoria."

The bridge lighting is another story. When the suspension cables were being spun, it was required that the operation, once started, be completed in a single construction season. Leaving the individual wires or strands of wires exposed to the winter furies at the Straits was unthinkable. High velocity November winds could distort carefully aligned wires which individually were only the thickness of a pencil. Also, contraction and expansion due to extreme temperature changes could cause inordinate rubbing and the thin, protective coat of zinc could be worn off, leaving the steel wires exposed to rust and erosion. Ice piled on the individual strands could cause stretching. No, the cables had to be completed before winter: the wires had to be laid out, bunched into strands of 340 each and then those into 37 strands (making a total of 12,580 wires squeezed into a 24.25 inch circle), covered with a protective lead paste, and then tightly wrapped in a circular fashion with cable wire. Thus, it became an around-the-clock operation. The chain link fence work platform, which followed the contour of the cables, had to be lit up for night work.

So it was that one evening during the summer of 1956 Dr. Steinman and Prentiss Brown were enjoying an evening stroll along the beach on Marquette Island where, about twenty miles east of the bridge, Brown had a summer retreat. As the sun sunk below the horizon the cable work lights glowed ever more brightly in the oncoming darkness. They both stopped to admire the diamond pendant hanging from the sky.

"Dr. Steinman," asked Brown, "how much would it cost to install permanent lighting on the bridge cables?"

Steinman thought a moment. "Oh, I would estimate about a hundred thousand dollars."

The next day Brown told me about about his conversation with Steinman and asked how we were doing on construction costs. I replied that barring any unusual incidents, there would be a substantial amount of money remaining in the contingency fund.

That started the chain of events that led to the installation of cable lights. The resident engineer noted my request for an estimate of their cost in his next daily report. The Steinman New York office, still working on the electrical contract specifications, made the necessary adjustments and fig-ured the cost thereof. The Authority at its next meeting unanimously approved the expenditure.

I knew that lights along the bridge deck to provide for safe night driving had long been specified, and I also knew that they would cast a bluish glow. When it came time to determine the appearance of the cable lights, I was told that there would be protective globes over the bulbs. Only clear or amber glass globes were available. Samples were brought to the office.

Several nights later the globes were rigged with bulbs, attached to a portable power plant, and taken out onto the bridge. Viewed from the shore, the clear globes cast off a white light; the amber, a yellowish or golden color. I was asked to make a choice. Which did I prefer, the amber globe or the clear globe? I visualized the bridge lighting with the deck casting its glow of blue and the cables bathed in yellow. There could be only one choice for a maize-and-blue alum-nus, class of 1934.

Power Plays and Politics

Any account of the behind-the-scenes activities that took place in connection with the Mackinac Bridge should include the two rather tawdry efforts to separate the chairman and the executive secretary from the Authority.

The first came in early 1969. The six-year terms of Prentiss M. Brown and Murray D. Van Wagoner had expired on June 30, 1968. Governor Romney had not announced their reappointment though there was no reason to think he would not. The incumbents continued to serve until replaced. Delays in making reappointments occur frequently, especially during and following election years. In the spring and summer of 1968 Romney was deeply involved in GOP presidential politics.

In retrospect, if we had been listening carefully, we might have suspected something was afoot. We had heard rumors that the person newly appointed to represent the state treasurer on the Authority had made some remarks in one of the local bars that he was going to get Brown and Rubin. We paid no heed to this until March 1969. Governor Milliken, who had succeeded Romney when the latter accepted a federal post, was asked at a press conference why

149

he had not reappointed Brown and Van Wagoner. He replied that he wanted to investigate some anonymous allegations that had been made about the chairman and Authority personnel, mainly Rubin. The question, if not the answer, was staged and had the desired effect: headlines ran in all media alleging bridge personnel of questionable behavior. Although the anonymous allegations had been in the governor's hands for several weeks, the question raised at the governor's conference was delayed until I was on a skiing vacation in Colorado.

A lengthy investigation followed. The allegations were described by the governor's own legal advisor as a "lot of Mickey Mouse stuff." Nevertheless, the attorney general's second deputy and top investigator spent several weeks interviewing bridge employees and residents of the St. Ignace area. Then he took about three months to compile his report. The upshot of all this was that some bridge employees were failing to follow the rules and regulations established for all state employees. The accusation was accurate. Since its creation, the Authority considered its operation separate from the state. Certainly that was not contrary to the intent of the legislature. All Authority revenues were deposited with the trustee, all purchases were made directly by the Authority and paid for by Authority check after approval by the consulting engineers, subject to immediate review by the trustee and quarterly audit by a representative of the state auditor general. These practices were pursuant to the provisions of the Trust Indenture, the contract with the bondholders. The investigation revealed no misfeasance, malfeasance, or dishonesty whatsoever. In a word, it was much ado about nothing. And that is what came of it.

The second attempt to get Brown and Rubin was not so clumsy as the first, but far less complicated. A bill was introduced in the state senate on July 23, 1971, to abolish the Authority. It was not difficult to obtain resolutions from northern Michigan organizations opposing the legislation. It appeared to those of us immediately concerned that there was little danger of the bill's passage, but having been burned once by failing to heed rumors, we decided to make all possible efforts to kill the bill. While in Lansing one day on some other matter, I asked my good friend Tom Farrell, a former newspaper man and an experienced hand around the capitol, for his advice.

"Where is the bill now?" he asked.

"In the Senate State Affairs Committee," I replied.

"Let's see," said Farrell. "That's Tony Stamm's committee. He's chairman and he's a good guy. Go see him."

I decided to take this advice. It was late in the afternoon. The senate was not in session, so I took my chances, hoping to find the senator in his office. I was seriously troubled, though. I had not had any opportunity to do any research on Senator Stamm, except that Farrell told me he was from Kalamazoo. This information lit a bright light in the dim recesses of my memory. Some thirty-three years earlier, in 1938 or 1939, the Michigan State Highway Department was planning to conduct a ceremony in Kalamazoo dedicating its newly widened main thoroughfare. As assistant director of public relations with the department, I was dispatched to make arrangements with the local officials. There was only one restriction placed on my mission. Under no circumstances was Anthony Stamm, the county sheriff and a budding politician of the opposite party, to be on the program. This was before Civil Service and present-day enlightenment. Both sides played the same way, so my restriction was not all that difficult to observe.

As I walked up the stairs to Senator Stamm's office I wondered if Sheriff Stamm and Senator Stamm were the same man. And if so, would he remember? I had never laid eyes on either of them. I nearly turned back. It was quite a gamble. I could figuratively get thrown out on my ear and would not have blamed him. But Farrell said he was a good man and my cause was right.

I introduced myself to his secretary and asked to see the senator. She replied that he was expected momentarily and invited me to take a seat in his outer office. This I did. I could no longer see his secretary nor the entrance to the senator's office, but I could hear any conversation unless it was whispered. Soon the outer office door opened, and I heard the secretary greet the senator. He asked if there were any messages. She responded and then told him that Lawrence Rubin was waiting to see him.

"Lawrence Rubin," he echoed, drawing it out as though delving deep into his memory. "Lawrence Rubin," I heard him say again, and feelings of despair came over me. "He remembers," I thought.

A few minutes later I heard him tell his secretary to send me in. As I shook hands with him I noted that he had difficulty getting up. One leg appeared to be stiff or disabled. Then I noticed a cane hanging from a coat rack behind his desk.

"Lawrence Rubin," he said, with that drawn out pronunciation, "I want you to meet my administrative assistant, Bill," and pointed to the young man seated close by.

"Bill," the senator went on, "let me tell you about Lawrence Rubin." Here it comes, I thought, as I vainly tried to frame a defense or an alibi, something.

"About thirty years ago, when I was a young punk still wet behind the ears, I was told there was a job waiting for me, if I went up to Lansing and applied at the State Highway Department. Well, I needed the job and when I got to the information desk I didn't know where to go or who to ask for. There was a fellow standing there, perhaps a few years older than I, who overheard my stumbling, awkward request. He came over to me, and literally took me by the arm and offered to help. He led me to the personnel office, introduced me to the director, and saw to it that I was in the right place. Well, Bill, that man was Lawrence Rubin."

Wow! I had no recollection of the incident whatsoever, but it certainly could have happened. The public relations office and information desk were part of the same operation, and the woman at the desk often did our typing. It would not have been unusual for me to overhear people making inquiries.

I confessed that I did not remember the incident when

the senator asked me, and then I added modestly that I was glad I had been of help.

"Well, Lawrence," he asked, "what can I do for you?"

I was glad to hear the "Rubin" omitted.

"Senator, there's a bill in your committee to abolish the Mackinac Bridge Authority."

"Oh yes, 1016," he said almost cutting me off. And then talking to both his assistant and me, he said, "Well, we have to have somebody up there running that bridge. I thought the Authority was doing a good job."

Before I could frame what I hoped would be a modest and tactful answer, he went on.

"I suppose we ought to have a public hearing," he remarked to his administrative assistant, and then he asked me, "Is there anything going on up there that might make a trip to the Upper Peninsula interesting and worthwhile?"

I thought a moment and replied that the I–500, the top snowmobile racing event of the season, would take place in Sault Ste. Marie during the first Saturday in February.

"Well, maybe we'll plan a hearing in St. Ignace in conjunction with it. Is that okay with you, Lawrence?"

"It certainly is, Senator, thank you very much."

With that we said our good-byes. The hearing was never held. Nor did Bill 1016 ever come out of committee.

Sheriff Stamm and Senator Stamm were obviously not the same person, though I suspect they were related.

24

Year-end Pieces

Many unusual and outstanding events occurred on and in connection with the Mackinac Bridge during its first twenty-five years of operation. I documented them each year in year-end pieces. The most interesting of these unusual happenings have been culled for inclusion herewith.

The overshadowing event of 1958 was the bridge dedication. As was related in an earlier chapter, this event should have been concurrent with the opening on November 1, 1957, but because November is on the verge of winter, the Authority decided to postpone the grand dedication ceremonies until the following summer, when the Straits area abounds in glorious sunshine and dancing blue waters. So what happened?

The sun shone and the waters danced like midsummer on November 1, 1957; the winds howled, waves peaked, and the skies opened up on June 26, 1958, the first day of the four-day dedication ceremony. Some sixty floats were practically ruined before the parade began; an army exhibit in Mackinaw City was flattened more effectively than if it had been battered by a superior enemy; the governor, scheduled to lead the parade, could not get to the mainland from Mackinac Island by boat, helicopter, or airplane. All that kept going through my mind as I watched the remnants of scores of bands and majorettes bravely marching in the storm was that famous line by Robert Burns that "the best laid schemes o' mice and men Gang aft a-gley."

The highlight of 1959 was the sailing of the yacht *Britannia* under the Mackinac Bridge with Her Royal Majesty Queen Elizabeth II aboard and accompanied by her consort Prince Philip. Thousands of persons flocked to the Straits on the forenoon of the scheduled event. British Security Service officials responsible for protecting the queen visited the Bridge Authority office several days in advance and requested that all traffic be stopped at the bridge towers while the *Britannia* sailed under the middle of the main span. I was willing to oblige but suggested that we hold up traffic at both ends of the bridge rather than at the towers. That would not do, countered the Britishers. They did not want to inconvenience anyone more than absolutely necessary.

Well, we followed their directions and stationed men at the main towers with instructions to stop all vehicular traffic upon receiving radio instructions to do so. What was not expected was a low-lying fog, especially dense east of the bridge, so that we could not track the *Britannia*. When the yacht was spotted as the fog bank lifted, she was about five hundred yards east of the bridge. The signal was given. Traffic was stopped. I suppose that in England proper Englishmen would remain in their cars, but this was America and hundreds of car occupants ditched their vehicles and ran out onto the center of the bridge waving and shouting for a look at the British royalty, especially Prince Philip. It must be admitted with some measure of shame that some persons threw small items such as coins over the side and there were even a few who spat.

Since the opening of the bridge hundreds of victims of agoraphobia have requested bridge personnel to drive their vehicles over the bridge. Agoraphobia has no respect for size, strength, intelligence, or courage. There have been burly truck drivers who have cowered under a blanket in the back seat of a patrol car while bridge personnel drove their trucks across. A jewelry salesman was a regular user of this service as he made his periodic trips to the Upper Peninsula. The most unusual case, though, was that of the vacationing doctor who made the trip north with some friends, but absolutely refused to go back over the bridge. He asked the supervisor on duty if there were any boat crossings. None were scheduled but one of the collector-patrolmen on his break overheard the request and volunteered to ferry the doctor across the Straits in his own boat when his tour of duty ended. He did not reveal that his vessel was a sixteen-foot aluminum boat with a ten-horsepower outboard motor. A deal was struck. In the meantime the wind revved up to about thirty-five miles per hour, and waves three to four feet high were rolling through the Straits. Well, they made it, but it would have been an infinitely safer trip over the bridge.

It may stretch one's credulity to be asked to believe that parents would take off for one side of the bridge or the other and leave their children behind. Yet it happened four times between 1958 and 1971. Always there was a quick and joyful reunion managed through the good offices of the bridge personnel. More than likely the parents and their children would recall the incident later in a somewhat jocular manner.

However, those who witnessed one particular incident in which someone was left behind would bet their paychecks there was no jocularity attached to it for a long time, if ever. It seems that at about 1:30 A.M., a couple driving north to Canada stopped in Mackinaw City for gasoline at a station about to close. The outdoor lights were being switched off. The husband, who was driving, decided to use the men's room, leaving his wife fast asleep in the backseat under a blanket. While he was away from the car, the wife awoke and decided to use the women's room. The husband returned to the car, paid for the gas, glanced at the blanket in the backseat, got in the car, and drove off.

Fortunately for him, the wife and gas station attendant had the presence of mind to call the Authority. The supervisor on duty radioed the Authority patrol car to pick up the distraught woman and transport her across to the fare plaza on the north side. He also alerted the fare collector in the northbound booth to query all male drivers. Traffic at that hour was light, so it was a simple matter to identify the driver who nearly went into shock when he discovered no wife under the backseat blanket. Waiting in the supervisor's office, he paced nervously back and forth until he was re-united with his spouse. The reunion was anything but joy-ful, however, and expletives and recriminations disturbed the quiet of the early morning.

Over the years a huge highway grader and a twenty-ton earth mover went out of control on the bridge. Luckily the steel bridge railing held. The damage was confined to some paint scrapings and bent railing and a couple of petrified drivers. The vehicle that nearly did make the plunge was a tractor-trailer combination with the stainless steel trailer car-rying about 44,000 gallons of milk. The driver was speeding far above the limit when his vehicle spun out of control. It skidded wildly, making almost a complete turn, but the rear end of the trailer hit the fence railing, which did not hold in this instance. The trailer came to a halt teeter-tottering out over the Straits. The tractor was still connected and re-sponded to the up and down movement of the trailer. The driver, almost in shock, was rescued, and so was the trailer, but not until all the milk was dumped out into the Straits. That year saw the best milk-fed fish catch in history.

One driver failed to notice that the camper on his pickup dropped off on the bridge. When he reached his destination eighty miles later, he called the State Police who had been alerted by the bridge operations supervisor. A chagrined driver returned to the bridge plaza where his camper was remounted none the worse for the the experience, although he had to endure the lost time, extra miles driven, and, no doubt, lots of good-natured ribbing.

Motorbikes, snowmobiles, and small single-axle trailers have been left behind inadvertently. One such trailer was carrying a small boat which did not look too seaworthy. When the cover was removed, it was found to be loaded with beer and whiskey. The "fishermen" who lost the trailer came bustling back to the bridge to pick it up and well that they did. There is just so much resistance that can be expected from bridge workers in view of such unguarded temptation.

Then there was the wallet with several hundred dollars found in a snow bank on the fare plaza several weeks after it was lost. It was returned to its owner intact, if somewhat worse for weather. On a much larger scale, the rear trailer of a double bottom combination broke loose on the bridge. The combination was northbound on the uphill grade. The trailer rolled backward until it hit the curb and fence railing and came to a halt. Fortunately it was empty. It usually carried twenty-five tons of stone. The tractor driver was unaware of the entire incident until he arrived at the fare plaza and the collector instructed him to go back for his "pup," the small rear trailer.

There have been several fatalities in connection with the bridge since its opening, but none relating to normal bridge traffic. Early on, a bridge crosser who appeared to be in good health was describing to his companion the beautiful view of the Straits from the bridge, when he keeled over the wheel. He was dead when the doctor arrived. In April 1975 a man apparently committed suicide by jumping off the bridge. A driverless van was found in the middle of the center span at 10:00 P.M., the motor running. In the van were a shotgun, a full box of shells, and a bottle of sleeping pills. The next morning evidence of somebody climbing over the bridge railing was discovered. The body was never found. The State Police did not close the case until 1982.

The worst tragedy involved three National Guard officers flying a private plane by the bridge. As members of a unit that had completed its training at Camp Grayling, they decided to check out the Straits area for possible winter maneuvers. Apparently, a thick fog disoriented the pilot. The plane was heard flying north, low and parallel to the bridge. Then, for some reason, at a height of about two hundred feet it veered west into the two-and-a-half-inch-thick suspender ropes some forty feet south of the north tower. Small pieces of the plane were found on the bridge deck. Paint marks were found on the suspenders on both sides of the deck. The plane plummeted into the Straits several hundred feet northwest of the north bridge tower. Watching the engine oil surfacing, the divers descending, and finally the recovery of the bodies was a highly emotional experience I will never forget. The accident took place on September 10, 1978.

There are two points about the bridge that deserve mention: one, the bridge has withstood all the violent weather of the Straits area—the winds, ice, currents, waves, downpours—and still stands just as solid and durable as the day it was built; second, all the principal, $99,800,000 in bonds, and all the interest, about $147,000,000, will be fully paid by the end of 1986, eight years ahead of schedule. It should be pointed out that since 1969, the legislature has appropriated $3,500,000 annually to the Bridge Authority as a subsidy to replace the loss of revenue due to a 60 percent reduction in fares. While this procedure did increase bridge traffic, it did reduce bridge revenues. When all the bonds are redeemed, the Mackinac Bridge Authority will be dissolved and the bridge will be operated by the Department of Transportation. The grants made by the legislature are scheduled for repayment by maintaining fares. However, what the legislature does, it can undo.

The Bridge Walk Tradition

Prior to the opening of the Mackinac Bridge on November 1, 1957, the Authority received many requests from individuals and organizations to be the first to do some zany thing while crossing the span. There were those who wanted to wheel a baby carriage, push a wheelbarrow, ride a unicycle, back a car, roll a hoop—any number of unusual stunts in connection with the bridge opening, except to jump off of it. For the most part, these requests were filed in the wastebasket, and the bridge opening ceremonies were models of decorum and dignity.

But one of them struck my fancy. It came from the International Walkers Association which proposed a walking race over the bridge as part of the dedication festivities in June 1958. It was about this time that walking as a recreation and exercise was becoming popular. Walks along the Potomac were the "in thing" among the nation's leaders in Washington, D.C. After I discussed this with Chairman Brown and staff members, we decided to permit the walking race. Two lanes of the bridge would remain open for automotive traffic, and two lanes would be reserved for walkers. So, on the foggy, rainy morning of June 25, a hearty group of sixty racers and non-racers, all members of the International Walkers Association, from several midwestern states, gathered at the south approach to the bridge in Mackinaw City. With professional seriousness, Governor Williams fired the starting pistol. Stopwatches clicked, and we all proceeded across the fog-shrouded bridge, legging it heel and toe for St. Ignace, five miles away.

My pleasure was diminished somewhat by trying to keep pace with the governor's long strides, even though he was not racing. At no time could we see more than fifty feet ahead, much less the water below, so thick was the fog. We could have been in a tunnel. But it was a gay gathering, with the jovial walkers—many of whom were health faddists—offering the governor and me wheat germ, black molasses, raisins, and other energy-building foods to carry us through the five-mile stretch. We made it in one hour and five minutes. The winner of the race made it in fifty-five minutes.

Although the weather was poor and there were few participants, it was fun. The idea of a bridge walk once a year appealed to me. The bridge was normally barred to pedestrians; and I had received many requests for permission to walk across it. With some apprehension as to whether or not it would turn out to be a successful promotion, I prevailed upon the Authority to announce the second annual bridge walk for Labor Day, 1959. The date was changed from late June to the end of summer because vacation travel dropped precipitously after the second week in August. We hoped that in due course, the bridge walk would become an attraction that would lengthen the season.

Formal racing classifications for men and boys and women and girls were added by the International Walkers Association. The total number of participants in 1959, racing and pleasure walkers combined, was about 250. This was a pretty good turnout, and plans were made for a bridge walk on Labor Day, 1960. Again the races, now sanctioned by the Michigan Amateur Athletic Union, were included, and contestants of national caliber participated along with 500 or so pleasure walkers. This gave us confidence that the bridge walk would become an established tradition.

There were 1,500 participants in the 1961 Bridge Walk and 2,500 in 1962. With this increase in participation, problems arose. Transporting all the walkers from one side of the bridge to the other, both before and after the walk, with only two busses, was impossible. Toilet facilities were not available to serve that many persons, especially on the north side. Heavy southbound Labor Day traffic was also delayed.

In 1963 the St. Ignace Chamber of Commerce made a stalwart effort to transport the 4,000 walkers to downtown St. Ignace in the hopes of relieving the demand for immediate southbound transportation. Nevertheless, many participants were forced to stand for hours in the rain on a water-soaked turf before one of the seventeen buses pressed into service could transport them back to their cars in Mackinaw City.

We received wholehearted cooperation from the communities surrounding the bridge in providing any and all buses available—from schools, airports, and private operators. At that time, we alternated the direction of the walk each year. However, the 1964 walk, which skyrocketed to 6,000 people, convinced us that the bridge walkers would be too much inconvenienced if the event were to continue in the northbound direction, because most of the bridge walkers originated in the Lower Peninsula and wished to return promptly after the walk. It was then that we decided the event would have to be southbound thereafter.

The Mackinaw City Chamber of Commerce arranged for local merchants to provide $1,500 worth of prizes for bridge walkers. Numbered certificates were presented to all walkers as they crossed the finish line, attesting to their participation. If a walker's certificate number corresponded to the number posted in a merchant's window, then a prize could be claimed. In addition to the fun and suspense of this promotion, a fairly accurate count of bridge walkers could be obtained.

The number of crossers increased in 1966, 1967, and 1968. More than 15,000 men, women, and children of all ages and descriptions enjoyed the festive holiday event. There were lawyers, doctors, teachers, mechanics, and ditchdiggers, grandmas and grandchildren hand in hand, boyfriends and girl friends arm in arm.

In 1966 Governor George Romney decided to walk the bridge, but he insisted upon walking with his bodyguards northbound and being greeted by the throng of walkers waiting to start on the north side. I accompanied him, pointing out interesting facets of the bridge such as the place where a driver had commented on the beauty of the bridge to his companion and then died of a heart attack—the first bridge fatality. I described the unusual design features of several foundations. I pointed to the separators on the vertical wire ropes which held up the bridge deck near the towers. These separators—steel braces shaped like figure eights—prevented the cable suspenders from rubbing during high winds. As we stepped over the three-foot-long finger-like expansion joints, I explained that they were necessary to account for the contraction and expansion of the bridge due to variations in temperature. Lengthwise, the bridge could expand and contract as much as twenty-seven feet.

We approached the halfway mark at a leisurely pace, when, running out of bridge trivia, I mentioned that he was the first governor to make the bridge walk since Governor Williams inaugurated it in 1958. Williams had made the crossing in sixty-five minutes. Romney demanded to know how far we had walked. I replied that we were halfway. He glanced at his wristwatch, muttered something about twenty-eight minutes, and took off as though he were jet propelled. Running after him, I realized he was determined to beat Williams's time. There was a press car ahead of us. I noticed that Romney was not quite keeping a heel and a toe on the ground, as is required by race-walking rules. Jogging alongside, I mentioned this to him since photographers were leaning out of the press car, clicking away.

"Governor, you're supposed to keep a heel and toe on the ground."

Without turning to me, he said, "I am!"

He beat Williams's time, finishing the walk in fifty-seven minutes—quite a feat, even though it was mostly downhill.

The governor proved that his 1966 performance was no flash in the pan by walking the bridge in 1967 in forty-seven minutes. He made no effort to better his time in 1968, when accompanied by Wisconsin governor Warren P. Knowles.

The 1969 Bridge Walk saw Governor William G. Milliken participate for the first time. He surprised a great many bridge walkers, especially those who chose to walk with him, myself included, by legging it across the bridge in fifty-one minutes. Until he started, it was expected that he was planning a leisurely walk, and I volunteered to accompany him, but before he had covered the first one hundred yards, it became clear that the governor was challenging Romney's time. However, many of the 16,000 bridge walkers wanted to shake his hand and take his picture, impeding his pace. The following year he went all out and set the all-time gubernatorial bridge-walk record of forty-six minutes and fifty seconds. This record still stands.

By 1970, there were more than 20,000 bridge walkers, occupying two lanes of traffic from 7:00 A.M. until noon. At the same time, southbound bridge traffic, vacationers returning downstate, were backed up for several miles along Interstate 75 and U.S. 2 west, because there was only one southbound lane available on the bridge. They were, with good reason, irritated and aggravated. They made their feelings known to the governor, the Bridge Authority, and the AAA headquarters in Washington, D.C., and Detroit with irate letters and telephone calls. Something had to be done. I decided to squeeze the bridge walkers, who by 10:00 A.M. were strung out sparsely along the bridge, from two lanes into one. My colleagues predicted that there would be all sorts of accidents with walkers and vehicles sharing the same side of the bridge. It did not happen. State Police opened the lane and the National Guard patrolled the walkers. There have been no accidents.

The bridge walk has not been without unusual incidents, some good and some not so good. For example, two marriages were performed one morning on the north anchor block, the huge concrete foundation holding the cables. One reporter described the nuptials as an event attended by 25,000 guests. Not all walkers participated, but those who did cheered and congratulated the two couples, who hopefully will have something to tell their grandchildren.

The American Agricultural Movement, an association of farmers disgruntled by the import of foreign meat products, tried to make a statement by tying up bridge-walk traffic. Somehow they managed to elude the police and drove their heavy farm machinery onto the bridge. They dumped foreign meat over the side and tried to embarrass Governor Milliken. If this were not bad enough, one of their number parked and locked his pickup in a manner which blocked all vehicular traffic.

Persons, for and against various projects, who did not interrupt the bridge walk or inconvenience walkers were welcome to publicize their programs. Nearly always, these promoters joined in the fun of the walk, and there would be lots of good-natured banter between walkers and promoters.

Then, there was the dog problem. Pet lovers were not at all happy when dogs, except Seeing Eye dogs, were banned from the bridge walk. Complaints and letters had been piling up in objection to the litter left by the animals, and action had to be taken. Not only was stepping in the refuse obnoxious, but it could be dangerously slippery.

There are always expressions of patriotism: bands, color guards, flag wavers, marching legionnaires. They all contribute to the color and character of the event. But the most dedicated of all was the young man from Wisconsin who made the walk on eight-foot-high stilts, wearing an Uncle Sam suit. His main problem was not the physical effort and strain imposed on his legs, but rather the wind, which if it had blown him over, could have given the Coast Guard below some lifesaving to perform.

The Coast Guard Auxiliary out of St. Ignace patrols the waters under the bridge just in case somebody gets careless or cocky when the National Guard personnel patrolling the bridge deck may not be looking. To date, nobody has toppled over a railing, but it remains a source of concern.

It is expected that participation in the Labor Day bridge walk will continue to grow. In 1983, seventy busses transported walkers to the starting line and then back to Mackinaw City. The certified count indicated that 42,000 walkers participated. At some point it will no longer be possible to accommodate all the walkers at one time. It may be necessary to schedule two walks on the same day or on different days. It is a problem with which the Authority will soon be faced, but it is the sort of problem the members will have pleasure in solving. The bridge walk has become a firmly established Michigan tradition and is recognized as the world's greatest walking event.

INDEX

Index

An advertising agency executive and writer, Lawrence A. Rubin has devoted much of his career to public service. In addition to serving as executive secretary of the Mackinac Bridge Authority, he has held the positions of executive director of the Michigan Good Roads Federation and assistant director of public relations of the Michigan State Highway Department.

The manuscript was edited for publication by Anne M. G. Adamus. The book was designed by Don Ross. The typeface for the text is Palatino, based on an original design by Hermann Zapf about 1950. The text is printed on 60-lb. Champion Publisher's Offset paper, and the book is bound in Holliston Mills Kingston Natural Finish cloth over binder's boards.

Manufactured in the United States of America.